Postmortem Fingerprinting and Unidentified Human Remains

Marzena Mulawka

Routledge
Taylor & Francis Group
LONDON AND NEW YORK

First published 2014 by Anderson Publishing

Published 2015 by Routledge
2 Park Square, Milton Park, Abingdon, Oxon OX14 4RN

and by Routledge
711 Third Avenue, New York, NY 10017, USA

Routledge is an imprint of the Taylor & Francis Group, an informa business

British Library Cataloguing-in-Publication Data
A catalogue record for this book is available from the British Library

Library of Congress Cataloging-in-Publication Data
A catalog record for this book is available from the Library of Congress

ISBN 978-0-323-26617-8 (pbk)

Postmortem Fingerprinting and Unidentified Human Remains

DEDICATION

This book is dedicated to the hundreds of thousands of unidentified and missing persons, as well as to their grieving families, who suffer many sleepless nights wondering about the whereabouts of their loved ones and continue their quest for the truth.

> "To the living we owe respect, but to the dead we owe only the truth." *(Voltaire)*

> "...I am waiting here
> Waiting for you to come home...
> If I wait it doesn't mean
> You will return..."
>
> *(Waiting by Norah Jones)*

DISCLAIMER

Any views expressed within this textbook are the author's alone and not necessarily those of the San Diego County Medical Examiner's Office, New York City Office of Chief Medical Examiner, or Federal Bureau of Investigation.

Names of commercial manufacturers are provided for identification only and inclusion does not imply endorsement by the San Diego County Medical Examiner's Office, New York City Office of Chief Medical Examiner, or Federal Bureau of Investigation.

ACKNOWLEDGEMENTS

My first thank you is to God, who allowed me a second chance to live and make the best of every day as if it is my last. A special thanks to my mother, who made me the strong woman I am today—*kocham Cię i nasze życie Mamuś, jesteś mój świat.* To my father, whose family dedication is immeasurable—*Tata, dziękuję że opiekujesz się tak bardzo nami.* To my sister, Małgorzata—thank you for sharing the best journey with me—life. Joe, Trish, Dr. Gruen, and Dr. Russevich—thank you for being the reason I still walk this Earth today to fulfill my calling of working in the Forensic Science field; you saved my precious life in 2010 and just three years later, look what I have been able to accomplish. Also a special thanks to the staff of University of Pittsburgh Medical Center, Family House, Baptist Sports Medicine, and New York University Department of Rehabilitation for helping me walk again. Chris, PIM staff, and Dave—I run again and walk like everyone else because of your help. To my family and friends—Zofia, Lucyna, Diana (and Perez, Sarna, Harris, and Haidos families), Deby, Todd, Abby, Mike (and Mosco family), Leeza, Lisa, Donell, Aaron, Shannon, Paul, Rachael, Shasta, Heather, Richard, Gary, Jeff, Josh, Mike, Dennie, Agnieszka, Gillian, Kat, Carou, Bridgette, Josie, Katie, and Urwis—you have helped shaped me into the person and professional I am today. Thank you for providing immeasurable support throughout a long journey in pursuing the field of Forensic Science and the hurdles I had to overcome in getting to where I am. I have never felt alone in this life thanks to all of you. Also, a special thank you to the entire staff of the San Diego County Medical Examiner's Office for their continued support throughout the entirety of this research, and the individuals who supported me at the New York City Office of Chief Medical Examiner. Ed—a special and sincere thanks for making the author-publisher connection possible and for your continued encouragement. In addition, a special thank you to the entire staff of the DHS Biometric Support Center and FBI CJIS Special Processing Center for all of their help and hard work in helping me to identify so many unidentified persons over these years from the West coast to the East coast.

CONTENTS

CHAPTER 1

Introduction

The ability to establish biological identity through forensic means is crucial to the identification of the deceased as pertaining to medicolegal investigations in the forensic and criminal justice communities. Scientific identifications—using modalities such as DNA and fingerprints—are always preferential to those using contextual means, such as personal effects or visual identification by a family member. During identification, antemortem and postmortem data are compared to confirm a positive identification if the two sets of data match with no inexplicable discrepancies. One of the most rapid, efficient, and cost-effective methods of forensic identification is fingerprint identification through comparing postmortem fingerprint records against antemortem fingerprint records. However, shortfalls in understanding the complexity of postmortem fingerprint processing and identification contribute to major national issues regarding the identification of unidentified human remains in the United States.

1.1 IDENTIFICATION OVERVIEW

In philosophical terms, identity is defined as the aspects of an entity that make it definable and recognizable, possessing unique characteristics or qualities that distinguish it from other entities. The meaning of identity, however, is more constrained as it relates to *biological identity* in the world of forensic science. Human identification as it relates to forensic science is grounded in the scientific disciplines of physics, biology, and chemistry—all of which are well defined and statistically verifiable (Thompson & Black, 2007). While some distinguishing attributes that establish biological identity are acquired prior to birth, such as fingerprints and DNA; other attributes are acquired throughout life, such as scars, tattoos, piercings, and dental intervention, to name a few. The ability to utilize these attributes to confirm and support human biological identity is crucial to the identification of the deceased in medicolegal investigations throughout the world. "Identification of an unknown body or a living person may be defined as a statement based on certain characteristics which correspond to those of a specific person, and that bodily characteristics are really the ones which determine with absolute certainty the identity of the body of a person" (Gustafson, 1966).

The ability to confirm and support human biological identity is crucial to the identification of the deceased as pertaining to medicolegal investigations. The requirements to establish the identity of the deceased fall into three categories—criminal investigations pertaining to unexplained deaths, accidents and mass disasters, and war crimes and genocide (Thompson & Black, 2007). This particular book will explore the first two categories in much more detail and depth than it will the last category. Furthermore, identifications can be divided into two categories: *tentative*—those in which there is an initial presumption of identity based on contextual evidence such as personal effects found associated with the decedent or a local missing person; and *unknown*—those offering no evidence as to the individual's identity.

The identity of the decedent can most often be accounted for when death occurs in a location such as an institution, hospital, or home; especially when the death was expected and due to natural disease and a physician is available to sign the decedent's death certificate. Family, friends, neighbors, or coworkers can easily confirm the identity of the deceased in these cases. However, visual or contextual identification methods are many times subject to error, especially during unnatural or unexpected deaths. Additionally, the forensic science communities have been steering away from visual and contextual identifications due to the prevalence of erroneous identifications that have occurred when scientific identification was not pursued. These erroneous identifications have occurred at local Medical Examiner/Coronor (ME/C)'s offices, such as the Van Ryn and Cerak mistaken identity case in 2006 (Lauer, 2009); as well as during mass fatality incidents, such as the Joplin Tornado disaster in 2011 (Bauer, 2011). For more information about these cases, go to http://www.nbcnews.com/id/23849928/#.UoKMdZTF2hM and http://www.kansascity.com/2012/05/20/3619904/joplin-coroner-its-about-being.html.

The identity of the deceased may be difficult to confirm due to many variables. Delayed discovery and recovery of remains or physically destructive forces can make visual identification difficult or impossible. Postmortem changes, such as decomposition, rigor mortis, or animal predation are only a few of the contributors to difficulties in identification. Deliberate alteration of visual appearance or possession of stolen personal effects—such as for financial gain, homicide, or other means—are other factors that may be involved in erroneous identifications (Thompson & Black, 2007). Moreover, even a visually identifiable deceased person can be difficult to identify if there are no missing persons matching the person's description available or no one is located who can visually recognize the person.

1.2 IDENTIFICATION CLASSIFICATION

Identification can be achieved through presumptive and positive identification methods using a combination of contextual and physical evidence. Presumptive identification methods do not identify characteristics that are unique to an individual and are not conclusive proof of identity. They display a series of general or class characteristics, which may exclude other individuals based on characteristics such as age, gender, race, blood group, height, etc. Traditionally, presumptive identifications usually involve visual recognition, personal effects, medical history, and a combination thereof that can establish a possible identification (Wagner, 1997).

Contextual evidence, also known as circumstantial evidence, includes associated personal effects, such as clothing and documents found with the body, as well as visual recognition by relatives, friends, neighbors, or coworkers of the deceased. While scientific means of identification are preferred within the forensic community, contextual identifications are routinely used by Medical Examiner/Coroners Offices in routine casework. This is mainly because contextual identifications, particularly the circumstantial evidence used to make these identifications, are more robust. In contrast, physical evidence includes medical information such as healed fractures, examination of external features such as tattoos or scars, and scientific information such as fingerprints, DNA profiles, and dental charting. Scientific evidence usually fulfills three requirements—it displays uniqueness and stability, and has been prerecorded as belonging to a known person (Thompson & Black, 2007).

Scientific identification methods are established when comparisons of antemortem (AM) and postmortem (PM) data yield similar characteristics that are considered unique to the individual, and no inexplicable discrepancies can be noted. These unique characteristics may include fingerprints, dental records, DNA profiles, anthropological data (i.e. healed fractures), and radiographic superimpositions (i.e. prosthesis, sinuses, etc.). The majority of positive identifications in medicolegal death investigations today are confirmed based on scientific evidence due to its accuracy. Credibility of confirming a positive identification tends to increase with the collection of matching these specific, unique data markers, especially when they include more physical than circumstantial evidence. In addition, although many medicolegal investigations differ on a case-by-case basis, positive identifications are always preferential to presumptive identification methods. Legally certifying an individual's identity most often occurs after a positive identification has been confirmed. Nevertheless, if a comparison is being performed, and various inexplicable inconsistencies are found that cannot be explained, the putative victim is excluded as the unidentified person. "Contrary to identification, elimination is the safe and ambiguous outcome of a comparison in that it permits a clear statement that these two descriptions do not originate from the same individual" (Keiser-Nielsen, 1970).

1.3 FINGERPRINT IDENTIFICATION OVERVIEW

> *"The palms of the hands and the soles of the feet are the very remains by which a corpse might be most surely identified, if impressions of them, made during life, were available" (Galton, 1892).*

A fingerprint is defined as a reproduction of the friction arrangement, whether in whole or part, of a human digit when its impression is deposited onto a surface (Figure 1.1a,b). Friction ridges are present on the palmar and plantar surfaces of the hands and feet; they allow humans to grasp objects with their hands and gain traction with their feet (Uhle, 2010). Friction ridge skin contains raised ridges and

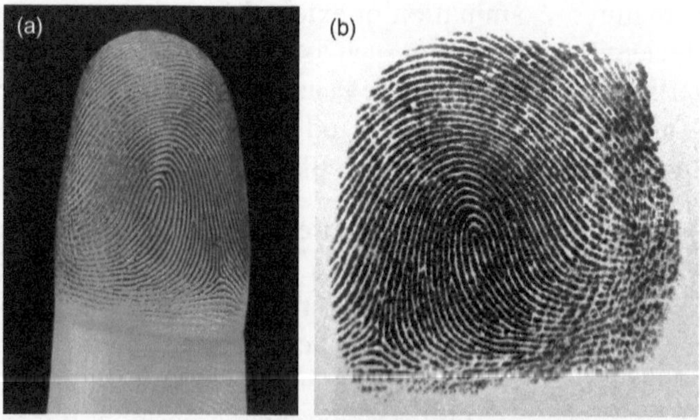

Figure 1.1a,b Friction ridge skin and its corresponding reproduction, known as a fingerprint.

recessed furrows that are composed of two main layers—the outer layer is known as the epidermis, and the inner layer is known as the dermis. The dermis contains dermal papillae, which create the raised portions of the epidermis on the plantar or palmar skin. A fingerprint impression is traditionally acquired from the epidermal friction ridge skin. However, the dermal papillae can be very useful for acquiring PM fingerprint impressions from decomposing remains. In general, the term "fingerprint" usually refers to impressions that are created with the pad on the distal portion of the digits. However, some fingerprint records contain impressions of other areas of the digits, palms, or feet, which have all been used to make identifications.

There are three types of fingerprint impressions—known, latent, and plastic. Known fingerprints are the intentional reproduction of the friction ridges from known fingers onto a fingerprint card or other medium. Latent fingerprints are two-dimensional impressions that can be visible or invisible at the time of deposition; both can be enhanced for visualization by utilizing chemical, physical, or electronic processing techniques. Latent fingerprints are created when eccrine glands present in the friction ridge skin deposit natural secretions onto a relatively smooth surface. They can also be created by contaminants, such as oil or blood, transferred from the friction ridges onto a surface. These are known as patent fingerprints, which can be visualized by the naked eye. Plastic fingerprints are created when a certain material, such as wax or putty, retains the shape of the ridge detail from friction ridge skin, creating a three-dimensional image of the friction ridge arrangement (Mulawka, 2008).

Fingerprint identification, also known as dactyloscopy, is defined as the process of comparing unknown and known impressions created by friction ridge skin in order to determine if they were created by the same source (Ashbaugh, 1999). These impressions can include impressions from fingers, palms, and toes. Despite the billions of human and automated computer comparisons that have occurred, no two fingers, palms, or toe impressions have ever been found to be identical when originating from different sources. Identification occurs when a certified fingerprint expert determines that two friction ridge impressions have originated from the exact same source to the exclusion of all others.

Although there is no exact date at which it was first used, the science of fingerprints can be traced as far back as the first century, when the Romans used a palm print to prove that an individual was framed for murder. In addition, many ancient cultures have used fingerprint impressions as a means for authentication. Moreover, hieroglyphics have been found that depict fingerprints and were acknowledged in ancient history, which may have set the stage for the scientific development of modern fingerprint identification (Uhle, 2010). During the nineteenth century, categorizing and classifying fingerprints became of significant interest, with Prussian professor Jan Evangelista Purkinje being one of the first to note their importance. Purkinje defined nine basic fingerprint types, followed by William Herschel, who acknowledged the individuality of fingerprints, using them to authenticate contracts. The first use of fingerprints in forensics occurred in Tokyo, when Dr. Henry Faulds used a handprint comparison to eliminate a suspect from being convicted of committing a crime, and later matched the print to the true suspect, who eventually confessed (Fisher, 2004; Lee, 2001). Dr. Faulds published a letter in the journal *Nature* (1880) that discussed his scientific observations regarding fingerprints and their identification potential. Soon thereafter, Sir Francis Galton published the book *Fingerprints* (1892), in which he described the individuality and persistency of friction ridge skin, providing empirical support to the underlying scientific principles of fingerprint identification (Uhle, 2010).

Before automated fingerprint technology revolutionized fingerprint searches, manual fingerprint classification systems were used to categorize fingerprints. Three classification systems—the Vucetich, Roscher, and Henry systems—predominated ten-print classifications. The Henry system, created in 1898 by Edward Henry, is based on discernible ridge patterns—the arch, loop, and whorl, each containing further subpatterns. The Henry system became widely adopted by law enforcement and forensic experts and is currently still in use by fingerprint examiners. It was used as a standard by the Federal Bureau of Investigation to create a national fingerprint repository, which became automated in the 1980s and was known as the Integrated Automated Fingerprint Identification System (IAFIS); IAFIS is currently being upgraded into a new system known as Next Generation Identification (NGI), (discussed in Chapter 6).

1.4 OVERVIEW OF UNIDENTIFIED HUMAN REMAINS IN THE UNITED STATES

As of 2007, approximately 40,000 sets of unidentified human remains (UHR) were being held in the offices of medical examiners or coroners

(ME/Cs) throughout the United States (Ritter, 2007). It is estimated that during any given year, as many as 4,400 UHR cases are investigated by ME/C offices, of which 1,000 remain unidentified and become "cold" cases (Hickman et al., 2004). On any given day, approximately 100,000 missing person cases remain active in approximately 17,000 jurisdictions across the United States. When examined over a significant period of time, these cases have accumulated to be in the 100,000s. Due to these enormous numbers that continue to accumulate with the passage of time, many experts have referred to this predicament as a "silent mass disaster over time" (Ritter, 2007). These cases are often forgotten and converted to cold cases due to limited resources and a gap in knowledge of techniques in forensic identification and investigation.

As of 2004, the Bureau of Justice Statistics estimated that more than half of the ME/C offices in the United States did not enforce policies for retaining records on UHR prior to disposition and burial. X-rays, DNA, and/or fingerprints were not retained from many of these cases and many UHR may have already been buried or cremated. Even with exhumation, a very costly process, there is no guarantee that there would be any remains available that are suitable for any sort of testing. DNA and x-rays may be possible to acquire; however, any ridge detail that may have been present on the fingers prior to burial may be gone, as the best chance of acquiring examination-quality fingerprints is when the body is in possession by the ME/C. Therefore, without retention of any specimens that can be utilized for further testing, chances of identifying these individuals are severely diminished, if not eradicated.

The rapid progression in forensic and scientific technology has allowed for the possibility of linking unidentified persons cases and unsolved missing persons cases by means other than investigative leads. Due to these technological advancements and the availability of funds within the United States today, one would infer that a consistency would exist among agencies that are tasked with the identification of UHR; however, the forensic identification process and availability of resources differ on national, state, and local levels. Many jurisdictions lack consistent procedures for pursuing the identification of UHR and missing persons. In addition, many ME/Cs and Law Enforcement Agencies (LEAs) continue to be unaware of the vast resources available to aid their investigations due to lack of information sharing. This only further impedes the efforts to solve these cases and link them to unsolved missing persons cases. As a result, families of these cases continue to wonder what happened to their loved ones and struggle with the agony of possibly never having the ability to lay them to rest (Mulawka & Craig, 2010a).

1.5 OVERVIEW OF POSTMORTEM FINGERPRINTING

As of yet, there has not been a consolidated resource delineating the multiple issues surrounding postmortem (PM) fingerprinting in the United States, while also providing an approach to address each issue, fingerprint techniques and combinations used for PM fingerprint processing, and a methodology for searching against antemortem (AM) fingerprint records. Although various fingerprinting techniques have been published and are currently used in many ME/C offices, many agencies continue to be unaware of the newly developed techniques and the avenues that can be pursued to facilitate searching against many available AM fingerprint records. If the most advantageous investigative methods and fingerprint techniques could be combined, a uniform procedure could be created to streamline and increase the effectiveness of the PM fingerprint identification process. The text will aim to address the following objectives:

- Educate the reader about the issues surrounding PM fingerprinting and propose a strategy to rectify many components to improve the fingerprint identification process.
- Delineate procedures regarding PM fingerprint processing and recovery of examination-quality PM fingerprint records from unidentified decedents or unverified decedents.
- Delineate a strategy and procedures to submit the aforementioned PM fingerprint records to the appropriate local, state, federal, and international agencies in order to perform an adequate and thorough search of all available fingerprint records to exhaust all efforts of fingerprint identification.
- Delineate a proposed strategy to manage unidentified PM fingerprint records and underline the importance of retention and resubmission.

If the law enforcement and forensic communities better understand the strengths and limitations of current fingerprint technology and resources available, as well as take measures to employ the aforementioned processes by searching against all available fingerprint databases and increasing federal submission capabilities, PM fingerprint identification will increase on a nationwide scale.

CHAPTER 2

Postmortem (PM) Fingerprint Processing Overview and Workflow

There are significant differences between antemortem and postmortem fingerprint acquisition, since recovering fingerprints from the deceased can prove to be quite cumbersome. During postmortem fingerprint recovery, the decedent's fingers may need to be reconditioned due to various stages of decomposition and other postmortem changes. There are various techniques employed during postmortem fingerprint recovery that require supplies and equipment that must be handled with caution. As such, universal precautions and donning personal protective equipment is imperative when operating in a biohazardous environment. Additionally, proper documentation and photography of the overall condition of the remains, as well as photographing the hands and the fingers, is necessary prior to starting recovery techniques. Forensic examiners should consult Uhle's three-step Deceased Processing Methodology for guidance on the recovery of examination-quality postmortem fingerprint impressions. In addition, the development of a postmortem processing workflow can facilitate decisions regarding which specific fingerprint techniques should be used.

2.1 ANTEMORTEM FINGERPRINTS VERSUS POSTMORTEM FINGERPRINTS

Contrary to popular belief in the forensic science community, there is a significant difference between postmortem (PM) and antemortem (AM) fingerprinting. Although their technical aspects may appear similar, fingerprint recovery methods for acquiring fingerprint records from the deceased (Figure 2.1a–c) can be much more challenging than obtaining fingerprints from the living (Figure 2.2a–c). When acquiring AM fingerprints, the living subject is manipulated against the medium. On the other hand, when acquiring PM fingerprints, the medium must be manipulated against the decedent. Additionally, if a living individual has an injury, such as a laceration, on the friction ridge skin, the AM fingerprint record can be recorded once the wound heals. On the contrary, the condition of

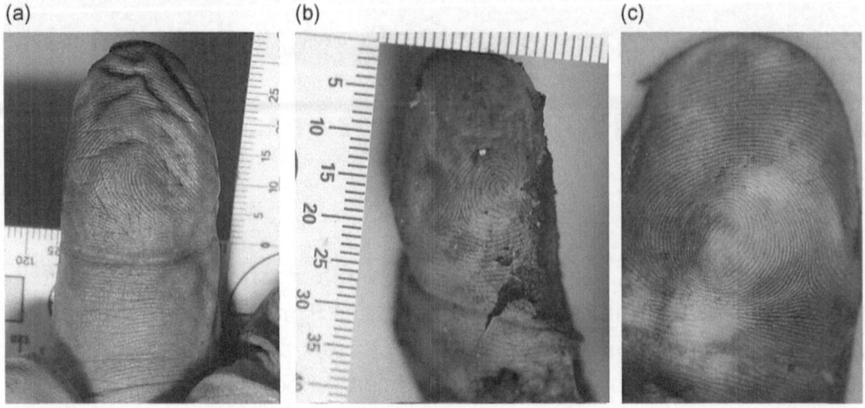

Figure 2.1a–c Friction ridge skin from deceased subjects (©NYC OCME 2012).

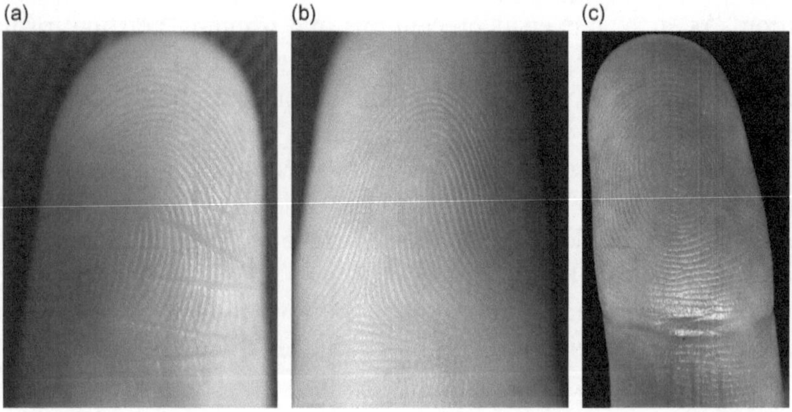

Figure 2.2a–c Friction ridge skin from living subjects.

PM friction ridge skin can be significantly compromised by various destructive influences due to the circumstances of death and/or severity of PM changes, such as rigor mortis, deterioration, and dehydration. As such, reconditioning techniques may need to be employed prior to recording the fingerprint impressions. The decedent's skin will never heal and its fragility must be evaluated during the examiner's initial assessment. The skin may be so fragile that the forensic examiner may have only one chance to capture an examination-quality fingerprint record before a significant portion of the scientific information is unsalvageable.

Because preserving, processing, and recording PM fingerprint records can present a significant challenge, forensic examiners should be properly educated and trained in the various basic and advanced PM fingerprint recovery techniques. Adequate skill, experience, patience, physical dexterity, mental composure, and determination are also necessary traits required for PM fingerprint processing due to the various levels of difficulty that each unique case may present. These traits will maximize the chances of capturing all available friction ridge information. Nevertheless, the successful development and recording of PM fingerprint records can be very rewarding to the forensic examiner(s) involved, as the minimal ridge information acquired may lead to the identification of an individual and could potentially accomplish the most important aspects of forensic identification—timely and accurate next-of-kin notification. Additionally, the identification of remains through fingerprints can also lead to solving an open homicide investigation.

2.2 DECEASED PROCESSING METHODOLOGY

Before examining the decedent, any documentation describing the condition of the body, as well as photographs, should be viewed, if available, because this may give the examiner an inclination as to whether basic or advanced fingerprint recovery techniques will be necessary and which techniques should be used. If the decedent is the victim of a mass fatality incident, learning the details regarding the location and nature of the incident may give the examiner an idea of the type of damage that may be observed on the remains. Aaron Uhle, Latent Fingerprint Examiner and Major Incident Program Manager for the Federal Bureau of Investigation Laboratory Latent Print Support Unit developed a deceased processing methodology (Figure 2.3) to guide and facilitate forensic examiners in the recovery of examination-quality PM fingerprint impressions (Uhle, 2010). In 2013, the author partnered with Mr. Uhle and colleagues to create a more in-depth fingerprint processing workflow diagram, delineating more detailed steps to follow when processing a decedent for fingerprints (Figure 2.4).

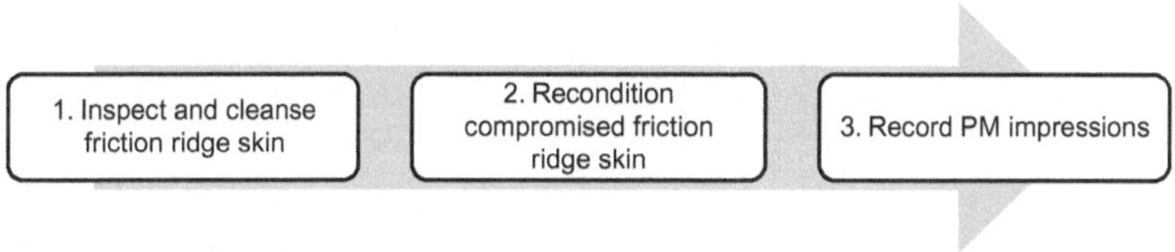

Figure 2.3 Deceased processing methodology.

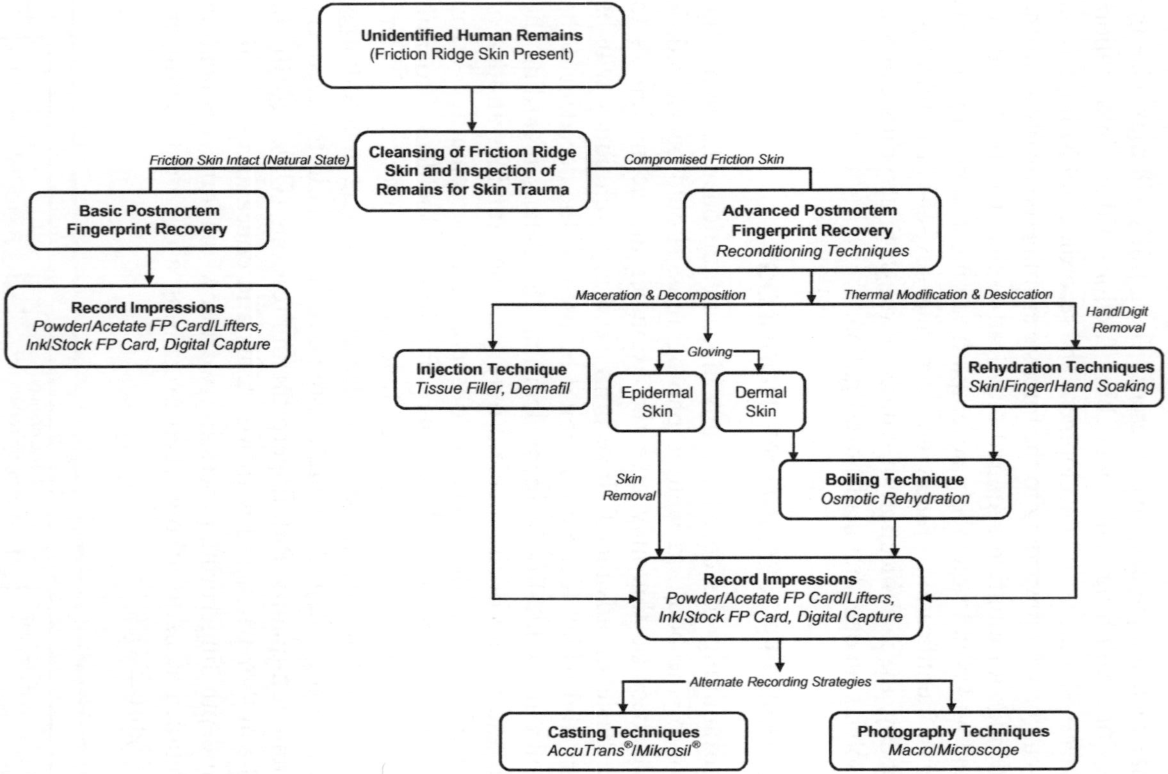

Figure 2.4 Postmortem processing workflow (Mulawka, Mosco, Uhle & Mokleby, 2013).

2.2.1 Personal Protective Equipment and Universal Precautions

Note: Before handling any human remains or biohazardous materials, the forensic examiner should ensure that personal protective equipment (PPE) is worn at all times. In addition, Universal Precautions should be used at all times. *Source:https://www.osha.gov/SLTC/etools/hospital/hazards/univprec/univ.html*

Fingerprint Acquisition PPE
Gloves (two sets)
Face mask/respirator
Eye protection/face shield
Gown/apron
Hair net
Shoe covers
Scrubs

2.2.2 Initial Photography and Documentation

Prior to any manipulation of the decedent's body or hands, photographs should be taken to document the overall condition of the body. Next, mid-range photographs should be taken of the hands, followed by close up (including scale) photographs of individual digits displaying any visible friction ridge detail. The examiner should have a physical or electronic form to document the entire fingerprint process performed. The form should at least include the following information:

Fingerprint Acquisition Form Information
Case number
Unknown or tentative name
Date of death
Gender
Fingerprint technician(s)
Date of fingerprint acquisition
Description of remains
Techniques used
Notes

All documentation and photographs should be clearly labeled with the case number and stored with the corresponding manual and/or electronic case file.

2.2.3 Step 1: Inspecting and Cleansing Friction Ridge Skin/Initial Assessment

The first step in PM fingerprint processing is visual inspection of the hands in order to perform an initial assessment to determine the quality of the friction ridge skin and if any damage has occurred (Figure 2.5). If the friction ridge skin is visible upon inspection and there is no rigor mortis present, the examiner may proceed to the third step and record PM impressions using basic fingerprint recovery techniques (Chapter 3). If rigor mortis is present, it is possible to break the rigor mortis by forcibly straightening the fingers by pulling each individual finger open. Additionally, pressing on the finger just above the knuckle area will cause the finger to straighten (Figure 2.6). Another method is to bend the wrist further toward the forearm and press on each finger close to the palm just above the knuckle area, which will cause each finger to straighten and separate from the rest of the hand. Finally, PM finger straighteners may be used to force the fingers away from the palm (Figure 2.7). If the aforementioned methods are unsuccessful, it may be necessary to dissect the tendons in the hand.

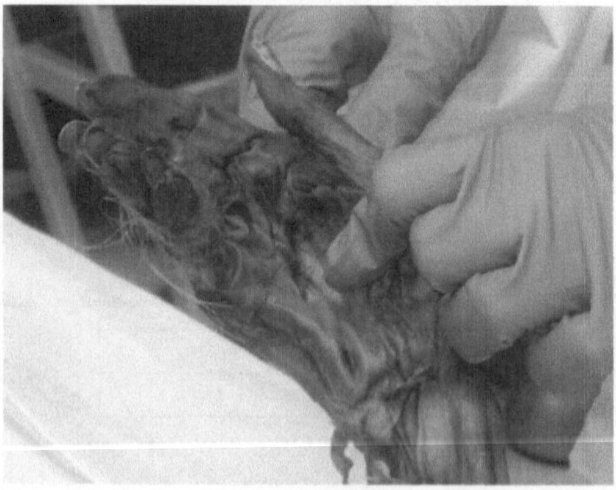

Figure 2.5 Inspection of hands for friction ridge skin (©NYC OCME, 2012).

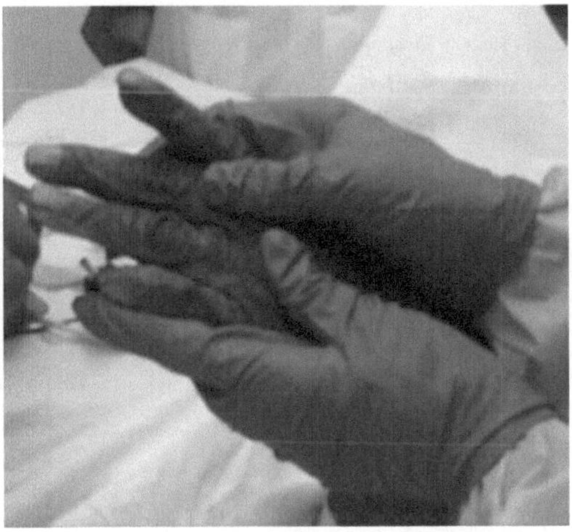

Figure 2.6 Straightening of hands exhibiting rigor mortis (©NYC OCME, 2012).

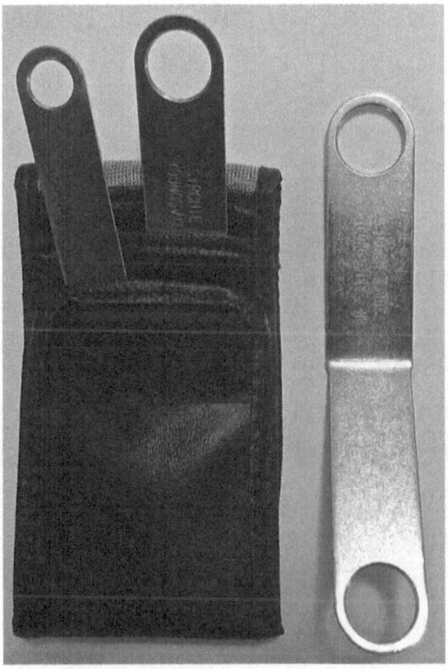

Figure 2.7 PM finger straightener kit.

2.2.3.1 Relaxation of Clenched Digit Technique

Note: Depending on the jurisdiction, there may be restrictions on cutting the decedent's tissue and advanced approval may be required from the medical examiner.

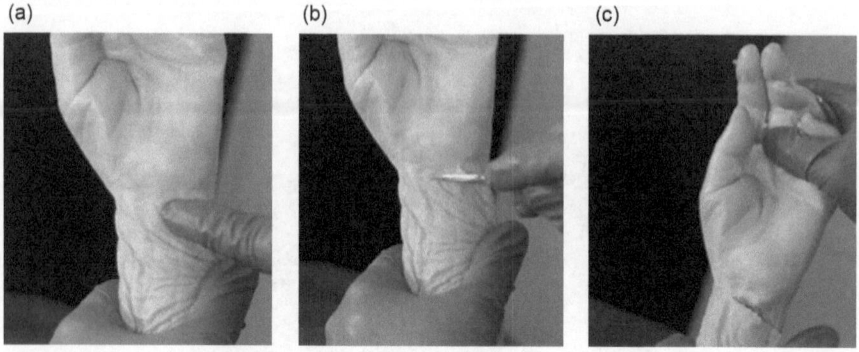

Figure 2.8a–c Relaxation of clenched digits in cadaveric hands (Reinecke, 2013).

Using a scalpel, make an approximately one-inch incision at the crease of the wrist just below the palm (Figure 2.8a). Be sure to cut through the skin and all underlying tissue (Figure 2.8b). After the tendons have been severed, digits 2–5 should be easily released from the clenched and flexed position (Figure 2.8c). In the event the digits still remain immovable, it may be as a result of incorrectly healed injuries or osteoarthritis finger injuries (Siwek & Reinecke, 2014).

Relaxation of Clenched Digit Techniques Supplies
#4 scalpel handle
#20 scalpel blade

2.2.3.2 Cleansing Friction Ridge Skin

If the hands are contaminated upon visual inspection, the examiner must first cleanse the hands in order to determine what techniques will be required to enhance ridge detail and record examination-quality postmortem fingerprint impressions (Figure 2.9a). Depending on the fragility of the friction ridge skin, the examiner must use discretion when cleansing to avoid compromising the skin's integrity. If the skin is intact, the hands can be cleansed using a soft paper towel or sponge and warm, soapy water—liquid soap[1] or bath wash[2] can be used for the soapy water (Figure 2.9b). If there is a significant amount of debris on the hands or the contaminant is dried and difficult to wipe off, the hands can be soaked for a few minutes in a shallow container of soapy

[1]The author has found Palmolive liquid soap to be most effective.
[2]The author has found Johnson's Bedtime Bath wash to be most effective.

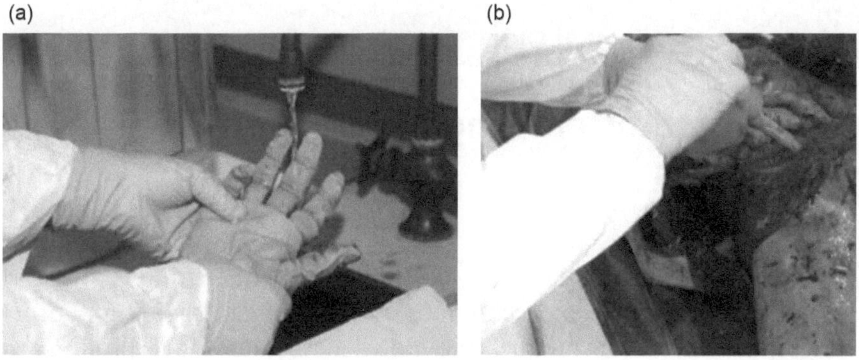

Figure 2.9a,b Cleansing friction ridge skin with water (©FBI, 2012).

water. Another method used is to coat the hands with the liquid soap or bath wash and cover the hands with a clear plastic bag. The bag can be tied or taped around the decedent's wrist to contain the moisture and left undisturbed for at least one hour. Additionally, a soft toothbrush can be used to remove debris from depressions or crevices in the friction ridge skin.

Cleansing Friction Ridge Skin Supplies
Soft paper towels or sponges
Liquid soap or bathwash
Shallow bucket/container
Plastic bags
String or tape
Soft toothbrush

Step 2: Reconditioning Compromised Friction Ridge Skin is discussed in depth in Chapters 3 and 4.

Step 3: Recording Postmortem Impressions is discussed in depth in Chapters 3 and 4.

CHAPTER 3

Basic Postmortem Fingerprint Recovery Techniques

Remains exhibiting undamaged friction ridge skin require the use of basic fingerprint recovery techniques, which include the Ink and Stock Fingerprint Card Technique, the Powder/Acetate Fingerprint Card/ Adhesive Lifter Technique, and the Livescan Technique. The latter method is preferred since it is a more efficient technique for postmortem fingerprinting. Before recording fingerprint impressions, drying techniques are necessary to eliminate moisture on the friction ridge skin and will reduce smudging of the resulting fingerprint impressions. Also, acquiring multiple postmortem fingerprint impressions is important in order to capture as much friction ridge information as possible. Lastly, the Putty Technique and its variations are useful to supplement the aforementioned basic techniques, capture friction ridge information within depressions, and streamline fingerprint recovery if a fingerprint technician is operating alone.

Basic fingerprint acquisition techniques are designated as techniques that do not require extensive training and are used on remains that exhibit undamaged and visible friction ridge skin. These techniques only entail the first and third steps of the Deceased Processing Methodology delineated in Chapter 2. In addition, these techniques do not require many fingerprint supplies and generally require less time to create an examination-quality postmortem fingerprint record.

In a 2013 analysis of 172 postmortem fingerprint cases requiring fingerprint acquisition at the New York City Office of Chief Medical Examiner, the frequency of basic and advanced postmortem fingerprint recovery techniques was observed and analyzed (Figure 3.1a). The use of basic postmortem fingerprint recovery techniques were required in 41% of all cases, while 59% of all cases required the use of advanced fingerprint recovery techniques (Mulawka, Mosco, Uhle & Mokleby, 2013). This percentage was then further broken down into the types of manual basic techniques used and their frequency (Figure 3.1b).

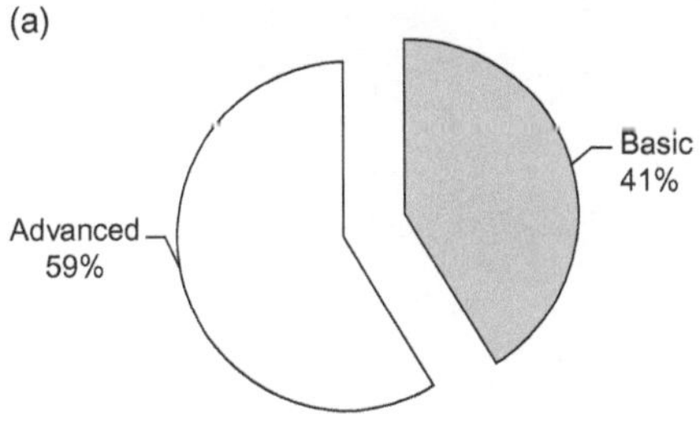

Figure 3.1a Use of basic versus advanced postmortem fingerprint recovery techniques on 172 cases at the NYC OCME (Mulawka, Mosco, Uhle & Mokleby, 2013).

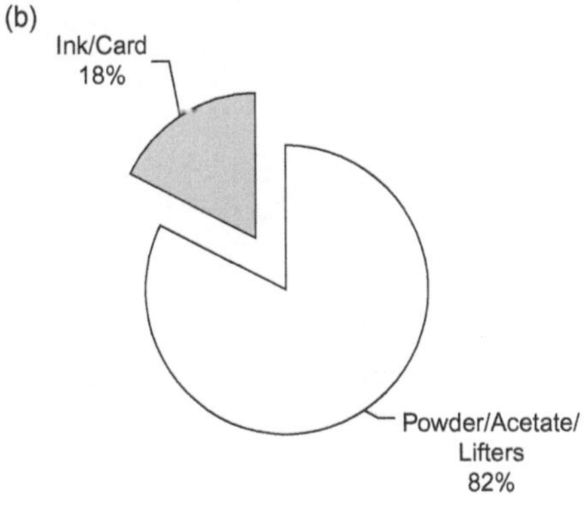

Figure 3.1b Use and frequency of basic postmortem fingerprint recovery techniques on 172 cases at the NYC OCME (Mulawka, Mosco, Uhle & Mokleby, 2013).

3.1 DRYING TECHNIQUES

Since the decedent may be fingerprinted after refrigeration of the body, condensation may form on the skin upon removal from a cold environment into warmer temperature. As such, the examiner must ensure that the fingers are dry before using basic techniques. This will prevent the fingerprint ink or fingerprint powder from smearing once it is applied to the acquisition medium. Depending on the degree of moisture, this can be achieved by blotting the fingers with lint-free paper towels or tech wipes that are moisturized by isopropyl (rubbing) alcohol or acetone (Figure 3.2). Depending on the fragility of the friction ridge skin, the examiner should use discretion with which solution to use—alcohol should be used on the more fragile skin and acetone can be used on non-fragile skin.

Caution: Any of the following techniques involving flame, heat, or electricity should be used away from alcohol, acetone, or any other flammable solutions.

The *flame technique* is another drying technique that involves the use of a butane grill lighter (Figure 3.3). The flame should be kept close to the friction ridge skin and lightly moved back and forth across the skin; the examiner should ensure not to char the skin. Another similar technique is the *light bulb technique*, which involves using a hot light bulb instead of the lighter, which will dry the skin using the same mechanism. Lastly, a hair dryer can be used to dry the skin; this is

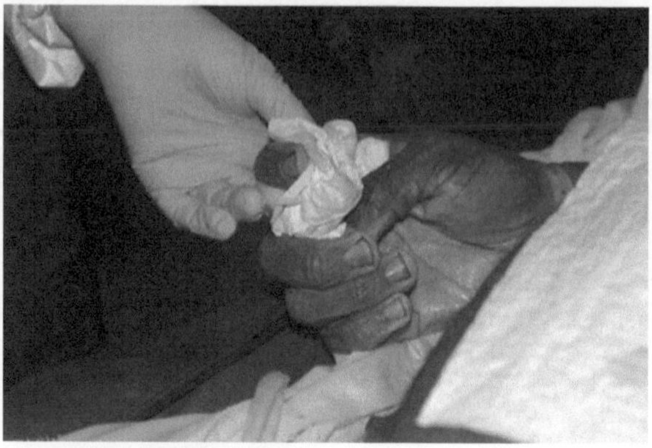

Figure 3.2 Finger blotting with tech wipes (©FBI 2012).

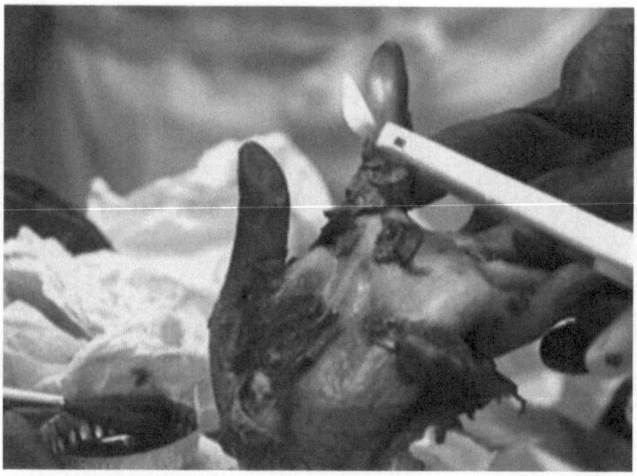

Figure 3.3 Flame technique (©FBI 2012).

known as the *hair dryer technique*. The hair dryer should be set on the lowest heat setting and moved back and forth at a safe distance from the skin until it is dry.

Drying Techniques Supplies
Isopropyl (rubbing) alcohol or acetone (only use alcohol on fragile skin)
Tech wipes or lint-free paper towels
Butane grill lighter (*optional*)
Light bulb and base (*optional*)
Hair dryer (*optional*)

3.2 IMPORTANCE OF MULTIPLE POSTMORTEM IMPRESSIONS

Due to the condition of the remains, there may be depressions or wrinkles in the finger that are still present even after reconditioning techniques are used. As such, the quality of an acquired postmortem fingerprint (Figure 3.4a) may not exhibit as much detail as an acquired antemortem fingerprint (Figure 3.4b). In order to collect as much detail as possible, multiple fingerprint impressions can be taken from the same finger (Figure 3.5a,b); this is especially important in cases when only a partial postmortem fingerprint impression is lifted. A qualified fingerprint examiner will be able to combine the information from multiple impressions of the same finger. It is important to clearly label each duplicated fingerprint impression on the fingerprint card (i.e. "9 L. Ring").

3.3 INK AND STOCK FINGERPRINT CARD TECHNIQUE

One of the first postmortem fingerprint acquisition methods developed was the ink and stock fingerprint card technique (Figure 3.6). The traditional ink-transfer method is usually successful; however, depending on the condition of the remains, it can be more difficult with rigor-stiffened, decomposed, or mummified fingers. As such, there are different variations of this technique. A small drop of fingerprint ink is deposited onto a spatula or flat surface (i.e. clear tape applied to a flat surface) and spread out using an ink roller. The spatula is then used to

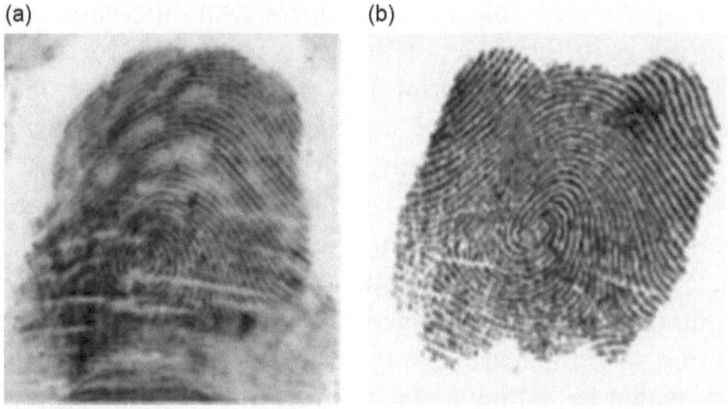

Figure 3.4a-b: Postmortem fingerprint impression and its corresponding antemortem fingerprint impression. (©NYC OCME 2012).

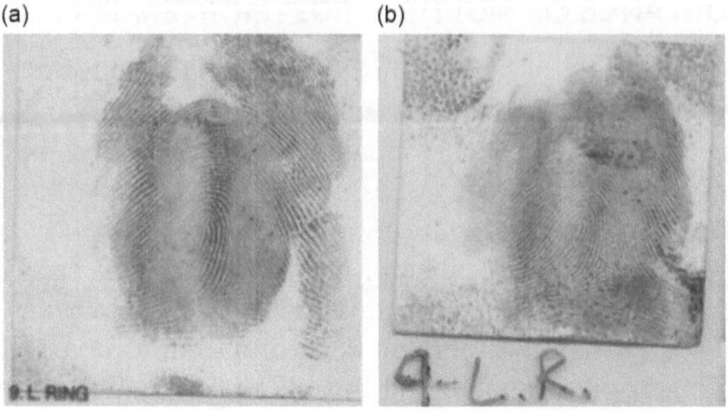

Figure 3.5a,b Multiple fingerprint impressions from the same finger (©NYC OCME 2012).

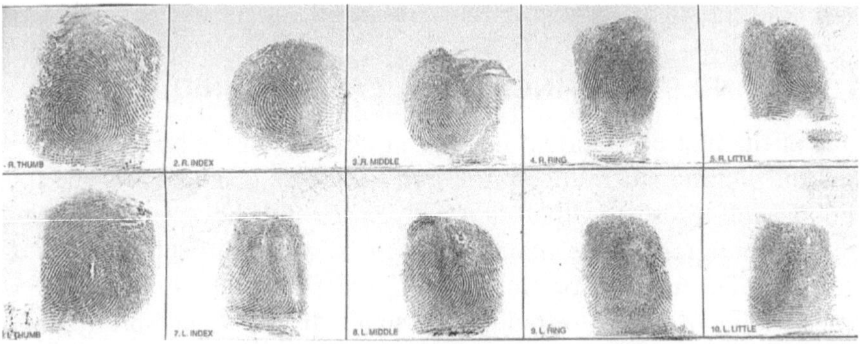

Figure 3.6 PM impressions using ink and stock fingerprint card technique (©NYC OCME 2012).

apply this specialized ink to the fingers. An alternate method of depositing ink onto the fingers is to use a regular size or small fingerprint ink pad; small fingerprint ink pads are easier to manipulate around each individual finger. Once the fingerprint ink has coated the finger, stock paper fingerprint cards are manipulated against the surface of the finger's ridge detail. The fingerprint card may be folded along the horizontal line separating the right hand from the left hand, which may make it easier to manipulate around the decedent's fingers. Another alternative is to use fingerprint card strips with a postmortem fingerprinting spoon (Figure 3.7a-c). Fingerprint card strips can be purchased or created by cutting a stock fingerprint card into strips. If a fingerprint impression must be retaken, printover tabs or address labels (cut to size) can be applied over the unacceptable fingerprint impression(s).

(a)

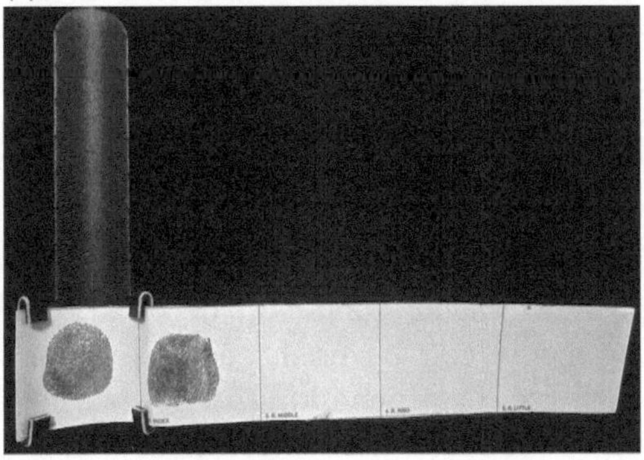

Figure 3.7a Postmortem fingerprinting spoon and fingerprint card strip.

(b) (c)

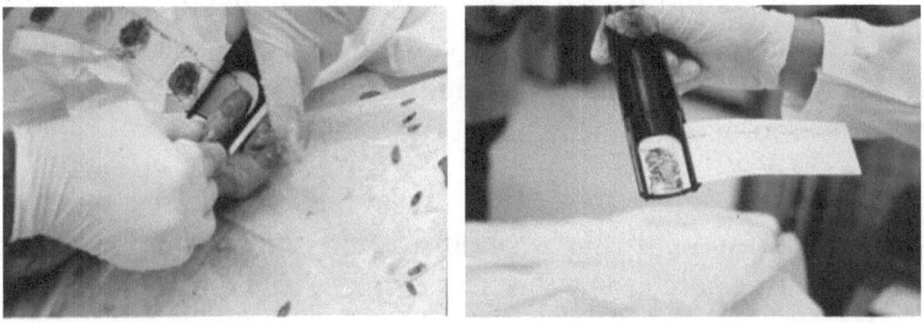

Figure 3.7b,c Postmortem fingerprint acquisition using fingerprinting spoon and fingerprint card strip (©FBI 2012).

Ink and Stock Fingerprint Card Technique Supplies
Isopropyl (rubbing) alcohol or acetone (only use alcohol on fragile skin)
White stock paper fingerprint card or fingerprint card strips
Fingerprint ink (ink pad, or ink/roller/spatula)
Tech wipes or lint-free paper towels
Black permanent marker
Fingerprint printover tabs or address labels
Postmortem fingerprinting spoon (*optional*)

3.4 POWDER/ACETATE FINGERPRINT CARD/ADHESIVE LIFTER TECHNIQUE

When working with the deceased, an alternative method to the ink-transfer method is using the powder, acetate fingerprint card, and adhesive lifter technique. This process creates a fingerprint impression that can be searched similar to fingerprint impressions created using the ink-transfer technique. A small amount of black fingerprint powder is deposited onto a weigh boat (or small shallow container) and a fingerprint brush (or foam paint brush) is lightly brushed against the powder. The decedent's dry fingers are then coated lightly with fingerprint powder (Figure 3.8). A transfer medium is then used to lift the fingerprint impression on the adhesive side of the medium. Different types of transfer media can be used, such as white adhesive lifters, frosted fingerprint tape, or white address labels cut to size. In order to prevent doubling of the fingerprint impression, it is imperative to contact the powdered finger only once with the adhesive side of the transfer medium. Once contact occurs, the rest of the transfer medium can be lightly pressed against the rest of the finger. The fingerprint lifter is then slowly lifted and placed onto the corresponding area on the ***backside*** of a clear acetate fingerprint card. The clear acetate fingerprint card can be created by photocopying or printing a regular stock fingerprint card onto blank transparent acetate sheets.

The aforementioned method is the author's preferred method for lifting fingerprint impressions because each fingerprint impression is acquired individually using this technique. The individual fingerprint lifters are easier to manipulate against the deceased, especially in cases where rigor mortis is present. Also, the adhesive lifter coupled with black fingerprint powder enhances the quality of the ridge detail and amount of information captured (Figure 3.9). Additionally, if the fingerprint impression lifted is not of a desired quality, it can be discarded and another one acquired without having to use printover tabs. Furthermore, the fingerprint lifters can be easily removed from the acetate sheet without damaging the lifter and the acetate sheet.

Powder/Acetate Fingerprint Card/Lifter Technique Supplies
Isopropyl (rubbing) alcohol or acetone (only use alcohol on fragile skin)
Tech wipes or lint-free paper towels
Black permanent marker
Acetate fingerprint card
Black fingerprint powder
Small weigh boat
Fingerprint lifters (size 1.5" × $1^7/_{16}$") or address labels (size 2" × 4" cut in half)
Fingerprint brush (squirrel hair, camel hair, fiberglass) or foam paint brush

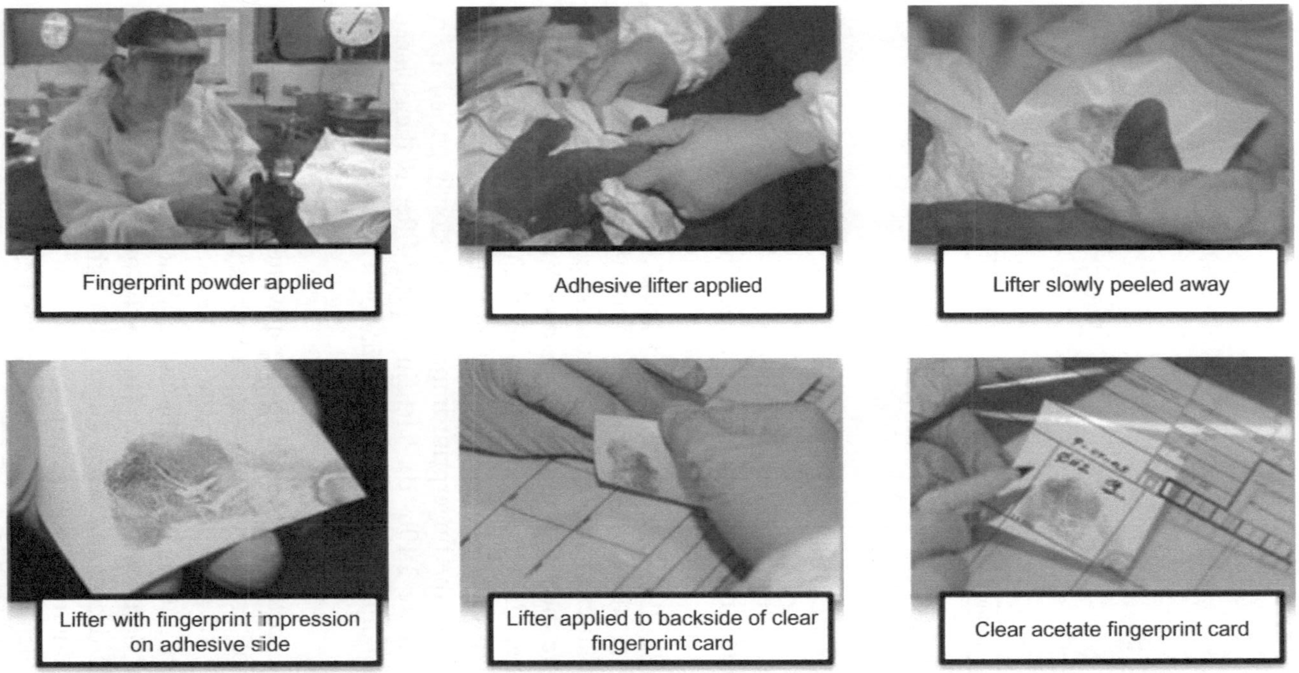

Figure 3.8 Steps for powder/acetate fingerprint card/adhesive lifter technique (©FBI 2012).

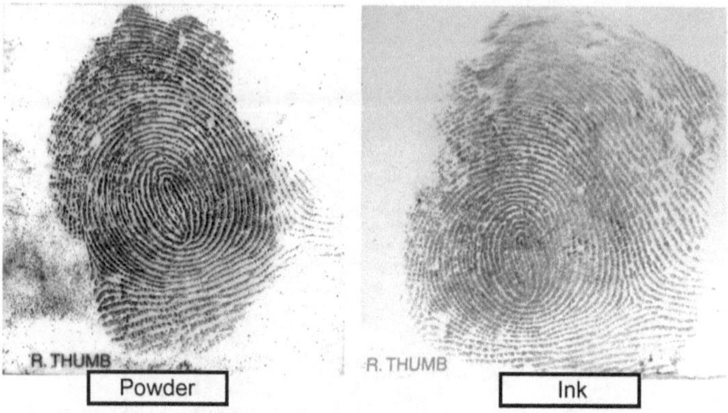

Figure 3.9 Powder fingerprint impression vs. ink fingerprint impression (©NYC OCME 2012).

3.5 PUTTY TECHNIQUE

When a fingerprint technician is working alone, the putty technique can be very useful and can supplement basic fingerprint acquisition techniques. There are different variations of this technique. A portion of air conditioning duct seal or plumber's putty is flattened to a 2.5 inch square that is about 0.5 inch thick. The adhesive lifter is then placed onto the flattened putty with the adhesive side facing up. The putty and lifter are then placed against the decedent's powdered finger with light pressure, allowing for the putty to slightly bend against the decedent's finger (Figure 3.10a). The putty and lifter are then removed and the lifter bearing the fingerprint impression is slowly peeled away from the putty (Figure 3.10b–d). The fingerprint lifter is then placed onto the corresponding area on the ***backside*** of a clear acetate fingerprint card.

An alternative to this method is to use a white latex glove swatch and ink instead of the fingerprint lifter and black powder. A square swatch is cut out of a white latex glove. The latex swatch is placed onto the flattened putty. A small amount of black fingerprint ink is applied onto the decedent's fingers. The putty and swatch are then placed against the decedent's inked finger with light pressure, allowing for the putty to slightly bend against the decedent's finger. The putty and swatch are then removed and the swatch bearing the fingerprint impression is slowly peeled away from the putty (Figure 3.11). The latex swatch is then placed onto the corresponding area on a

(a)

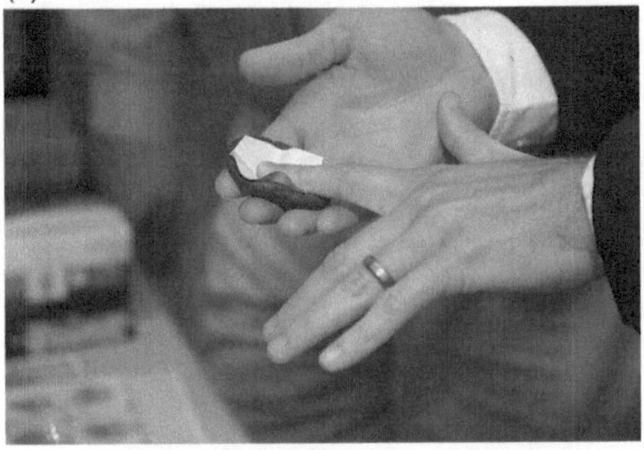

Figure 3.10a Putty technique used with lifter and black powder (©NYC OCME, 2012).

(b) (c) (d)

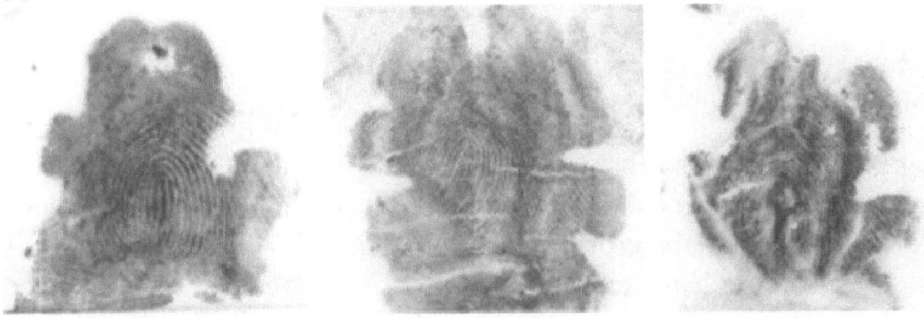

Figure 3.10b–d Fingerprint impressions on lifters using the Putty Technique (©NYC OCME 2012).

fingerprint stock card or onto the ***backside*** of a clear acetate fingerprint card and taped secure along the edges. Either variation of the putty technique is especially useful when the remains exhibit depressions in the friction ridge detail that are still somewhat pliable. The putty conforms to the depressions and will capture ridge detail that may not have otherwise been captured by an adhesive lifter (Figure 3.12).

Putty Technique Supplies
All supplies from Ink and Stock Fingerprint Card Technique or Powder/Acetate Fingerprint Card/Adhesive Lifter Technique
Air conditioning duct seal or plumber's putty
Scissors
White latex glove cut into swatches
Tape

Figure 3.11 Fingerprint impression on latex swatch using Putty Technique.

3.6 DIGITAL FINGERPRINT CAPTURE USING THE LIVESCAN TECHNIQUE

Research and advancements in technology have significantly improved fingerprint acquisition through electronic media and capture of digital representations of fingerprints. Since the early 1970s, fingerprint sensors have been advancing that can capture a "livescan" digital fingerprint image directly from a finger without the manual use of ink or fingerprint powder coupled with an acquisition medium. Digital capture devices have also become smaller and more mobile, streamlining fingerprint acquisition. Additionally, computer algorithms have been developed to automatically process digital fingerprint images (explained in Chapter 5).

Increasing workload and caseload at Medical Examiner and Coroner (ME/C) Offices has demanded a faster, less costly, and more efficient solution for fingerprint acquisition. As manual postmortem fingerprint acquisition is time-consuming, costly, and cumbersome, some ME/Cs have started to use livescan devices to streamline the process. Digital fingerprint capture has proven to be a very expedient and inexpensive method of positively identifying the deceased. Although digital fingerprint capture technology will continue to advance and most likely replace the manual basic postmortem fingerprint recovery process, it is important that fingerprint technicians remain knowledgeable in manual fingerprint recovery techniques for situations where the

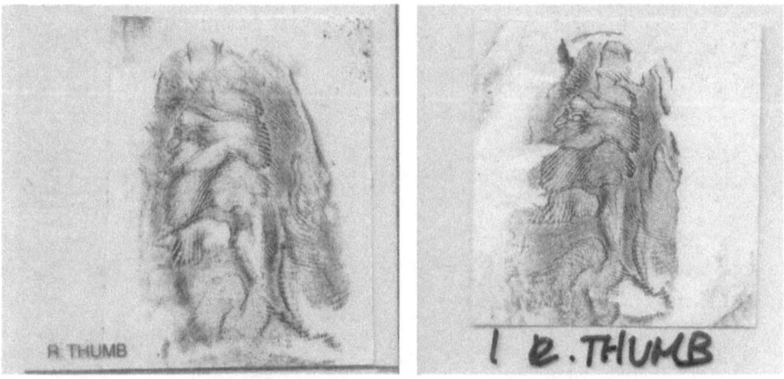

Before Putty Technique After Putty Technique

Figure 3.12 Fingerprint impression before and after using Putty Technique (©NYC OCME 2013).

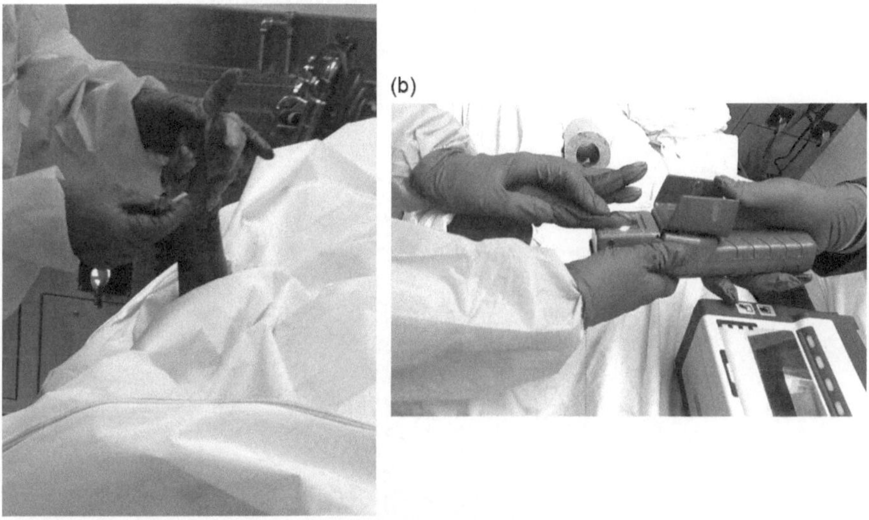

Figure 3.13a,b Drying of fingers and placement on livescan platen (©NYC OCME 2012).

digital fingerprint capture device may not be working properly or is unavailable.

The livescan method is very successful on remains that exhibit undamaged and visible friction ridge skin, as well as minimal rigor mortis. However, depending on the condition of the remains, digital fingerprint capture can be difficult or impossible in certain situations. The larger the livescan device, the more difficult it may be to capture examination-quality images from the decedent. The fingers must be dried before they are placed on the platen (Figure 3.13a,b). A major

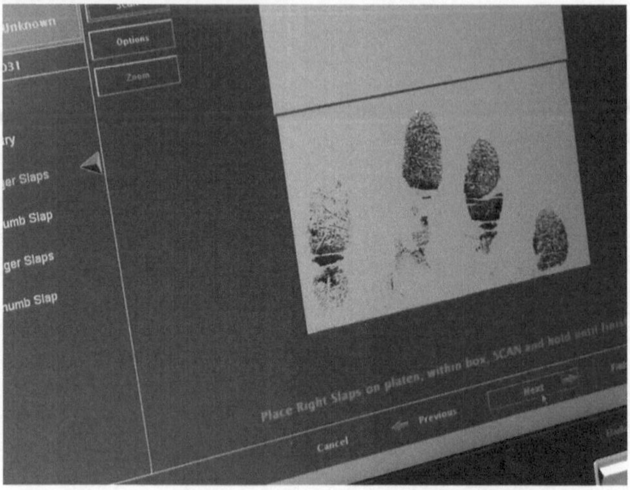

Figure 3.14 Real-time capture screen displays fingerprint capture (©NYC OCME 2012).

Figure 3.15 Real-time capture of examination-quality fingerprint impression.

benefit of using this method is the real-time capture screen that displays the information being captured as the fingerprint impressions are being acquired (Figure 3.14). Once contact occurs, the device must be manipulated against the surface of the finger to capture as much friction ridge information as possible. The livescan software will designate if the image captured is of acceptable quality or must be rescanned (Figure 3.15). The fingerprint technician must still use discretion and may have to manually override the software to rescan the impression if the image is accepted by the software, but the technician feels that capturing a better-quality image may be possible. The livescan software will guide the technician through the process of capturing each individual fingerprint image and once all ten images are captured, the software will display a digital ten-print card populated with all acquired images.

CHAPTER 4

Advanced Postmortem Fingerprint Recovery Techniques

Research in various advanced methods for fingerprinting the deceased has significantly advanced; however, the attempt to improve the quality of an acquired postmortem fingerprint record is a continuous process. Due to the challenge of manipulating the recording medium against the deceased, acquiring fingerprint impressions can be an arduous process, especially when dealing with remains exhibiting significant postmortem changes. A multitude of reconditioning, preserving, and recording methods have been published in various scientific journals, books, and magazines; however, the literature is often limited and dated. In addition, there has not been one consolidated manual or book delineating a modern workflow containing all advantageous reconditioning and recovery techniques, as well as when to pursue each specific method. The following chapter will assist forensic examiners in the successful recovery of examination-quality postmortem fingerprint impressions from damaged friction ridge skin. Unlike antemortem fingerprint processing, each case of postmortem fingerprint processing may require a unique combination of basic and advanced techniques due to the unique set of circumstances surrounding an individual's death. Recovered remains may exhibit damaged friction ridge skin that may be due to fauna (animals and insects), water (maceration), fire (charring), and weather (cold, heat, humidity). As such, the condition of the friction ridge skin on each finger will dictate which method must be used to successfully enhance and record any valuable friction ridge information; multiple techniques may be used on each finger and can differ considerably.

Advanced postmortem fingerprint recovery techniques are designated as techniques that require moderate to extensive training and are used on remains that exhibit damaged and poorly visible friction ridge skin. These techniques include all three steps of the Deceased Processing Methodology and are delineated in the Postmortem Processing Workflow described in Chapter 2. In addition, these techniques may require a substantial amount of fingerprint supplies and a significant amount of time to create an examination-quality postmortem fingerprint record.

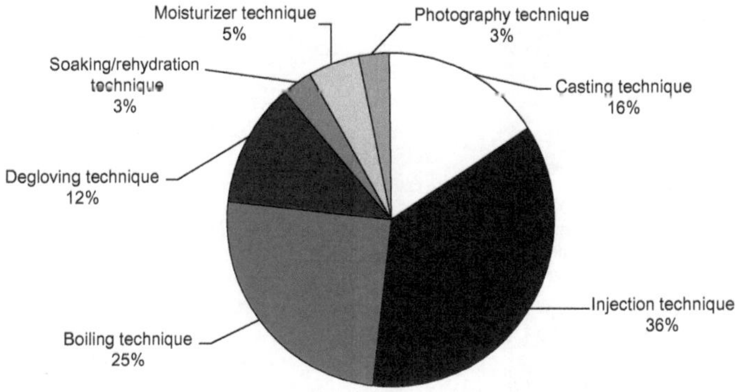

Figure 4.1 Use and frequency of advanced postmortem fingerprint recovery techniques on 172 cases at the NYC OCME (Mulawka, Mosco, Uhle & Mokleby, 2013).

In a 2013 analysis of 172 postmortem fingerprint cases requiring fingerprint acquisition at the New York City Office of Chief Medical Examiner, 59% of all cases required the use of advanced postmortem fingerprint recovery techniques (Mulawka et al. 2013) (Figure 3a in Chapter 3). This percentage was then further broken down into the types of advanced techniques used and their frequency (Figure 4.1). The statistics supported the importance of using and combining various advanced techniques when acquiring postmortem fingerprint impressions.

4.1 MACRO PHOTOGRAPHY/MICROSCOPE TECHNIQUES

Prior to using any techniques that may deteriorate the friction ridge skin, any visible friction ridge detail should be photographed. This can be achieved through digital photography. Use of a digital single lens reflex (DSLR) camera with macro lens, mounted on a copystand, is the preferred method, as the camera is portable and the field of view is adjustable. Alternatively, if the friction ridge detail being photographed is separate from the remains (i.e. castings, skin, fingers, etc.) a dissection microscope with digital camera attachment can also be used. However, the microscope is not as portable as the DSLR camera and the field of view may be much more limited (Figure 4.2a-c). The appearance of ridge detail can be further enhanced with the appropriate selection of direct, reflected, oblique, or transmitted lighting. Duel gooseneck lighting can provide the direct and oblique lighting, while a portable X-ray film illuminator viewer can provide the transmitted lighting. In addition, an

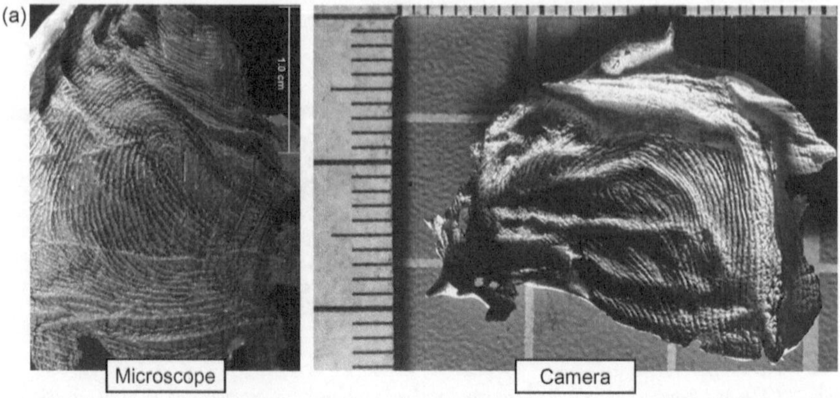

Figure 4.2a Mikrosil® casting photographed under dissection microscope and Mikrosil® casting photographed under DSLR camera (©NYC OCME 2012).

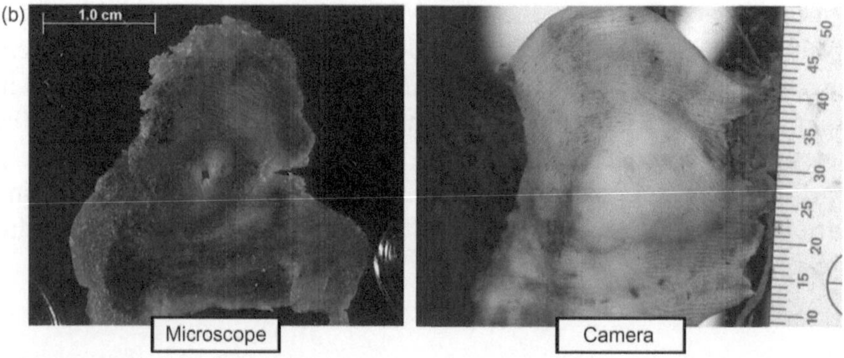

Figure 4.2b Epidermal skin photographed under dissection microscope and epidermal skin photographed under DSLR camera (©NYC OCME 2012).

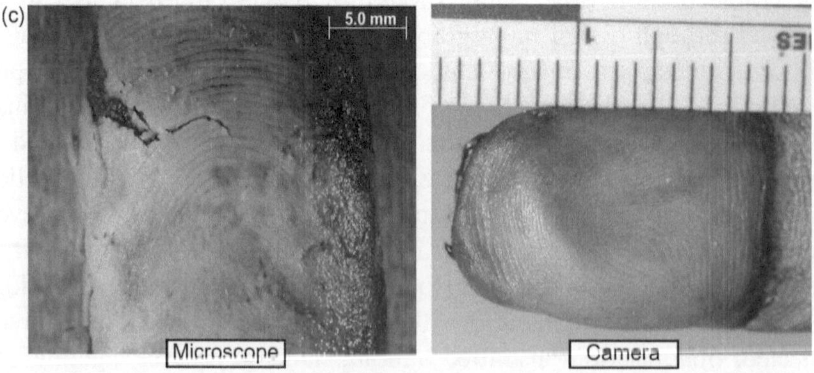

Figure 4.2c Finger photographed under dissection microscope and finger photographed under DSLR camera (©NYC OCME 2012).

alternate light source (ALS) can be used for more advanced photography of the fingerprint impressions (Marin & Buszka, 2013). It is also crucial to capture the images of friction ridge skin at 1:1, since the photographs will be compared to antemortem impressions of the same size. Otherwise, a photomographic scale should be included in the photographs so the image dimensions can be corrected through digital imaging software or a graphics-editing program such as Adobe Photoshop®.

Macro Photography/Microscope Technique Supplies
Photomacrographic scale
Digital single lens reflex (DSLR) camera with macro lens, external flash, and copystand or dissection microscope with digital camera attachment
Dual gooseneck lighting
Alternate light source (optional)

4.2 CASTING TECHNIQUE

The casting technique is an advanced recording technique used as an alternative transfer medium to the adhesive lifters used during the powder, acetate, and lifter technique. The casting technique is very useful when working with a decedent exhibiting desiccation and mummification, where the friction ridge skin is hard, significantly dry, and is not pliable. The casting technique can also be used after the rehydration technique. In addition, it can be used during a mass fatality incident when fingerprints need to be recovered rapidly and the rehydration method is not an option.

During postmortem changes, excessive drying of the skin leads to multiple depressions within the friction ridge skin that cannot be flattened. Application of adhesive lifters will not capture the friction ridge information within the depressions (Figure 4.3). Since the casting material is very pliable at the time of application, it will capture friction ridge information that is available on a flat surface, as well as within any depressions (Figure 4.4a,b). This process creates a three-dimensional fingerprint impression that can be flattened into a two-dimensional fingerprint impression, scanned or photographed, and then searched similar to fingerprint impressions created using the ink-transfer technique or the powder, acetate, and lifter technique.

Mikrosil® and Accutrans® are silicone-casting compounds often used for capturing tool mark impressions and latent prints at crime scenes, but

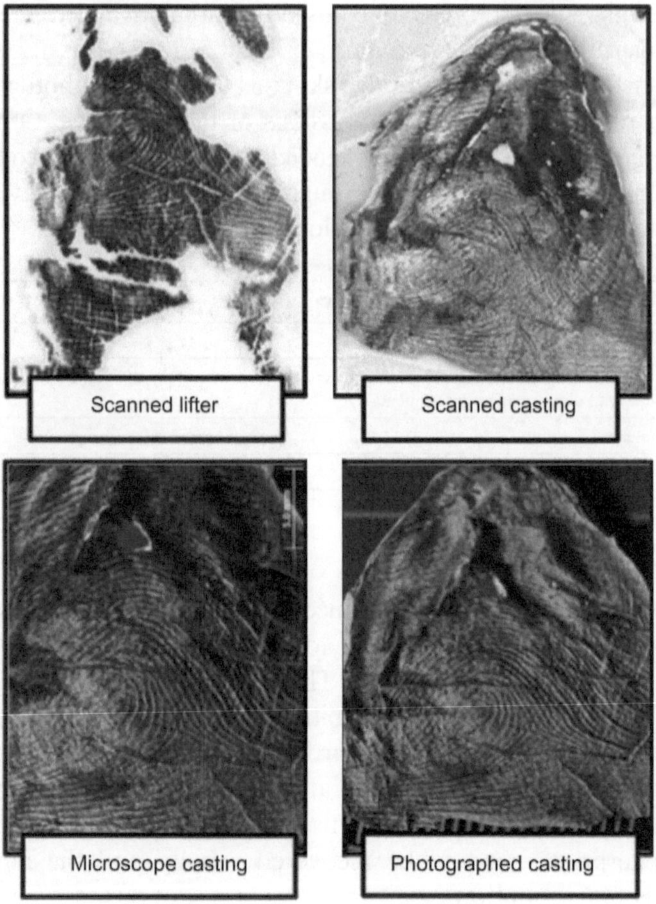

Figure 4.3 Fingerprint impression on adhesive lifter and fingerprint impression on castings from finger exhibiting multiple depressions (©NYC OCME 2012).

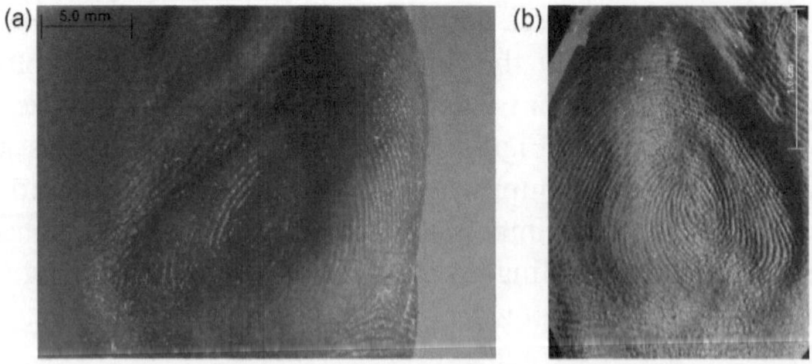

Figures 4.4a,b Photographs of finger exhibiting multiple depressions in friction ridge skin and resulting casting (©NYC OCME 2012).

are now commonly used for postmortem fingerprint acquisition. The decedent's fingers should be separated to avoid the castings from touching one another and sticking together. This can be achieved by weaving paper towels or tech wipes between the fingers. A small amount of black fingerprint powder is deposited onto a weigh boat (or small shallow container) and a fingerprint brush (or foam paint brush) is lightly brushed against the powder. The decedent's dry fingers are then coated lightly with fingerprint powder and casting material is then applied.

Mikrosil® requires a two-part formulation: one tube is larger, has the consistency of toothpaste, and contains the base material; the smaller tube contains a blue-colored catalyst, which hardens the base material when both are mixed with one another (Figure 4.5a). An approximately 2" strip of base material is squeezed onto a weight boat, followed by an approximately 1.5" strip of the blue catalyst. A wooden spatula or tongue depressor can be used to mix the two components together for about twenty to thirty seconds until the color of the blue catalyst is no longer visible in the base material. The mixing time must be kept to a minimum, since the material begins to harden after about thirty seconds (Figure 4.5b). Accutrans® is a polyvinylsiloxaine casting agent that also requires a two-part formulation; however, the product is in the form of an automix gun that allows direct application to the fingers using a spreader tip (Figure 4.6).

The casting material is immediately applied to the powdered finger. It is best to apply the casting material in one smooth "swipe" from one side of the finger to another. Once contact occurs, the rest of the casting

Figure 4.5a Mikrosil® materials.

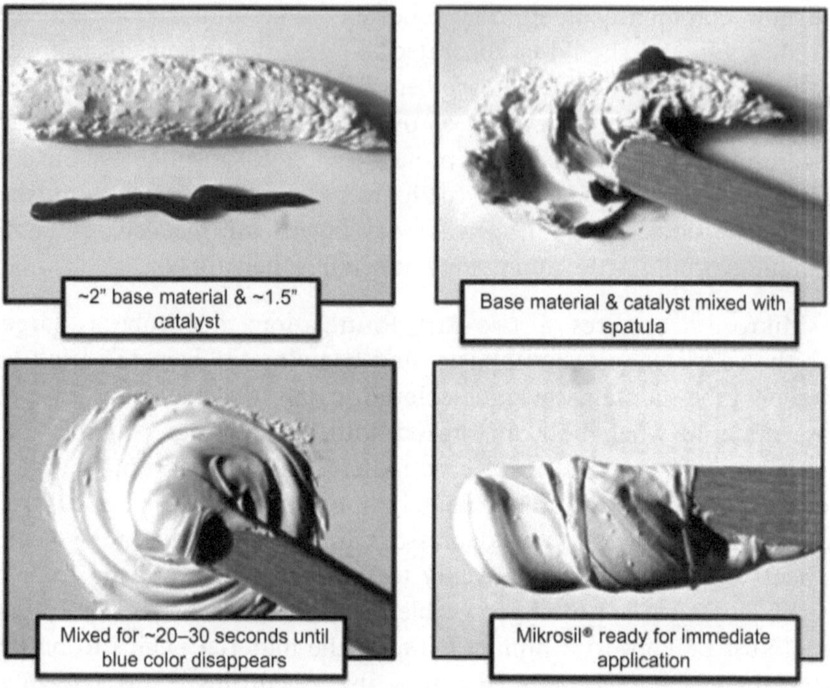

Figure 4.5b *Mikrosil® mixing steps.*

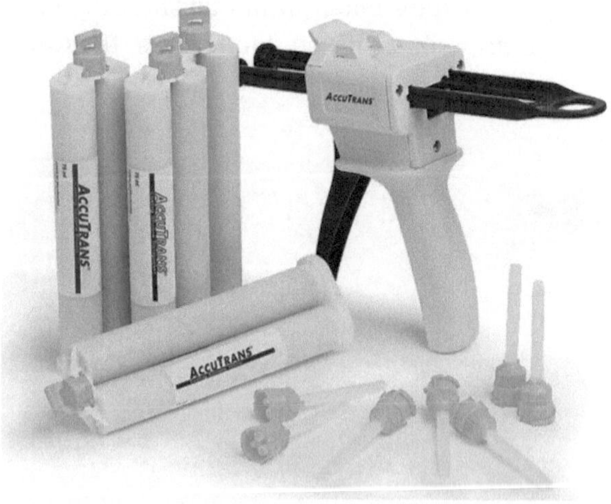

Figure 4.6 *Accutrans® materials (http://www.crime-scene.com).*

material can be lightly applied against the rest of the finger with the spatula. It is best to apply a thin coat so the resulting hardened casting can be flattened and captured as a two-dimensional image. The casting material should be left on the fingers for approximately ten to fifteen minutes. If using Mikrosil®, once the fingers are coated with the casting material the spatula can be returned to the weigh boat. The spatula can be checked periodically and if the material in the weigh boat is dry, the castings on the fingers will be dry as well. Once the material has dried, the fingerprint casting is then slowly lifted to reveal a "high contrast, highly detailed, three-dimensional mold" (Tomboc & Shrader, 2005) (Figure 4.7). The casting can be placed onto the corresponding area on the ***backside*** of a clear acetate fingerprint card or placed into a small, resealable clear plastic bag and marked accordingly. Each casting should be removed one at a time to avoid confusion.

When the castings are applied to the back of a clear acetate fingerprint card, clear tape or white address labels can be used to affix them to the back of the card. In order to ensure the castings are secure on the card, a large adhesive lifter (size 8" × 8") can be placed over the backside of the acetate fingerprint card covering the castings. The acetate card is then placed onto a flatbed scanner and scanned into a digital fingerprint image (Figure 4.8). The resulting castings depict friction ridge details in black and are in the correct orientation for comparison to antemortem records.

If the postmortem fingerprint card containing scanned castings is not identified, more detailed photographs of each individual casting should be taken with a scale (Figure 4.9a). This can be achieved by using a DSLR camera with macro lens and external flash or a dissection microscope with a digital camera attachment, coupled with dual gooseneck lighting (explained in more detail in Section 4.1). Individual photographs should then be imported onto a fingerprint card with the scale visible (Figure 4.9b). This can be achieved by using a graphics-editing program such as Adobe Photoshop®. The fingerprint card containing casting photographs should be resubmitted for a ten-print search and individual photographs should be submitted for a latent-print search; this will ensure thorough searching of the postmortem fingerprint record.

When the skin is severely damaged and there is limited friction ridge detail visualized on the white castings, fluorescent powder—such as

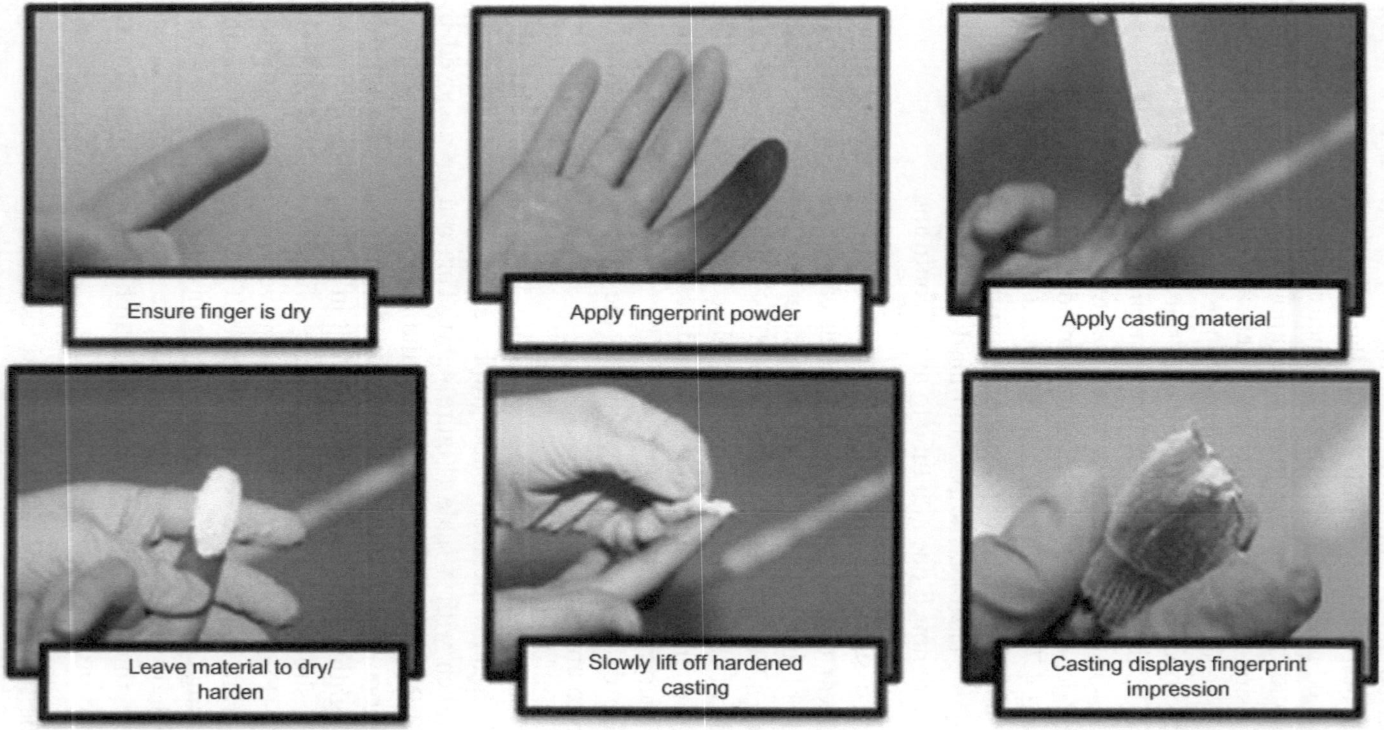

Figure 4.7 Steps for Casting Technique (©FBI 2013).

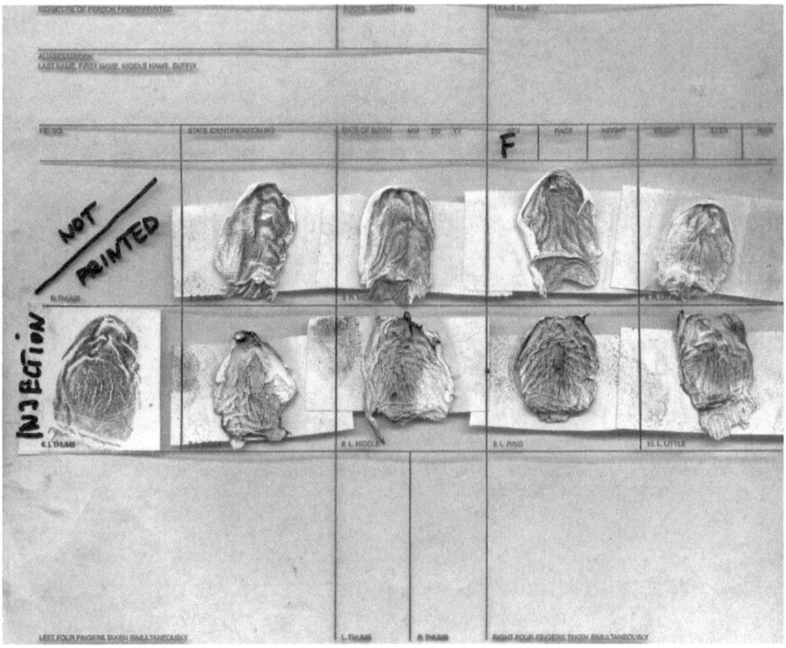

Figure 4.8 Digital fingerprint image of scanned castings (©NYC OCME, 2012).

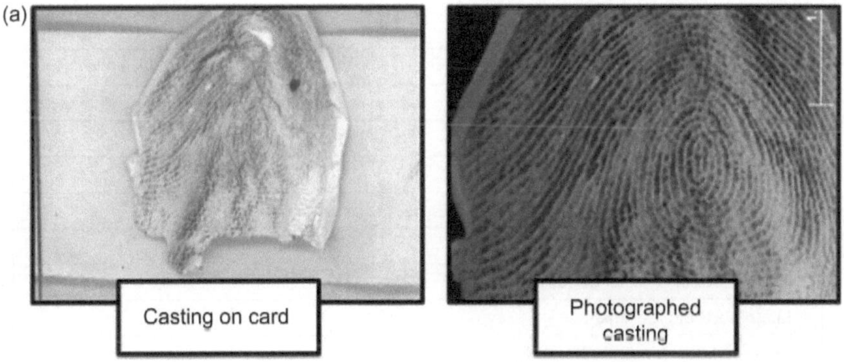

Figure 4.9a Scanned and photographed casting from finger exhibiting multiple depressions (©NYC OCME 2012).

Greenwop powder—and black casting material can be used. Greenwop powder fluoresces under ultraviolet light, so the resulting castings can be photographed under ultraviolet lighting (Tomboc & Schrader, 2005). If another fluorescent powder is used, the castings can be photographed using an alternate light source. If the resulting castings continue to

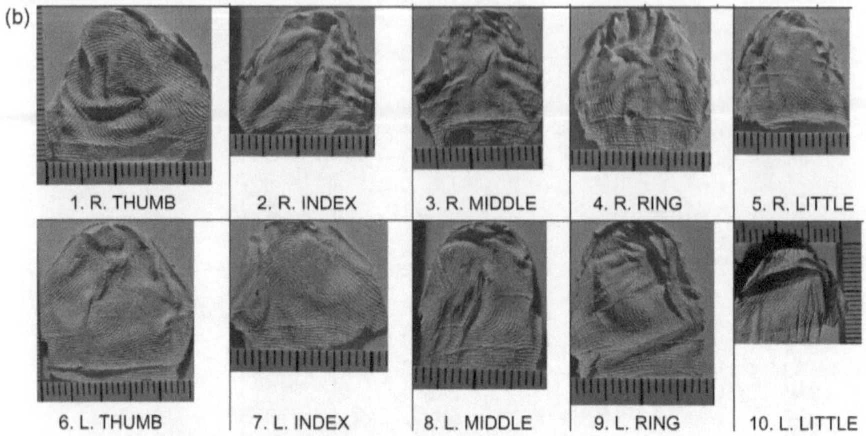

Figure 4.9b Individual casting photographs imported onto a fingerprint card (©NYC OCME 2013).

display low-examination quality friction ridge detail, the soaking and rehydration method should be used. Once the skin is rehydrated and pliable, the casting method should be attempted again to record examination-quality fingerprint impressions.

Casting Technique Supplies
Isopropyl (rubbing) or acetone (only use alcohol on fragile skin)
Tech wipes or lint-free paper towels
Black permanent marker
Acetate fingerprint card (a stock fingerprint card can be used to photocopy onto blank acetate sheets)
Black fingerprint powder
Small weigh boats
Fingerprint brush (squirrel hair, camel hair, fiberglass) or foam paint brush
White Mikrosil® or Accutrans®
Tongue depressor or small wooden spatula
Address labels or clear tape
Fingerprint lifters (size 8" × 8")
Small (2.5" × 3", 4 mL) resealable plastic bags
Photomacrographic scale
Digital single lens reflex (DSLR) camera with macro lens, external flash, and copystand or dissection microscope with digital camera attachment
Dual gooseneck lighting
Alternate light source (optional)
Greenwop or fluorescent fingerprint powder (*optional*)
Black Mikrosil® or Accutrans® (*optional*)

4.3 INJECTION TECHNIQUE

During postmortem changes, prolonged exposure to water or a moist environment leads to maceration and decomposition of the friction ridge skin. This creates wrinkles or creases in the fingers and deterioration of the epidermis. The Injection Technique is an advanced fingerprint recovery technique used when working with a decedent exhibiting friction ridge skin that is loose and wrinkled. In order to obtain examination-quality fingerprint impressions, the wrinkles and creases must be minimized or eliminated. It may be possible to carefully pull or pinch the skin taut to remove the wrinkles or creases and use basic recovery techniques with extreme care. If this method is unsuccessful, a liquid can be injected into the fingertips to elevate any depressed areas caused by the wrinkles or creases.

Various solutions can be used for the Injection Technique, such as water, saline solution, isopropyl alcohol, acetone, Dermafil®, Dodge Metaflow®, tissue builder, or glycerin. Dermafil®, Dodge Metaflow®, tissue builder, and glycerin not only fill out the wrinkles in the finger, but they also add firmness to the finger. Alcohol and acetone are the preferred method when working with decomposed remains that are very moist, as both solutions will serve a dual purpose—filling out the wrinkles and drying the skin. Acetone should not be used if the skin is fragile. Acetone, alcohol, and tissue builder—a viscous liquid used in embalming—should not be used around any sort of heat source (i.e. lighter used during flame drying technique) since they are flammable. A syringe is filled with one of the aforementioned solutions and the skin is slowly injected in the medial phalange, or first joint. When inserting the syringe, the examiner should ensure the angle of the needle is parallel with the finger to stay as close to the surface as possible, but also avoid puncturing any area of the friction ridge skin. If the friction ridge skin is punctured, the liquid will leak out of the puncture site and it will be impossible to keep the friction ridge area dry for successful recording. Once the skin is penetrated, the needle tip should just pass under the distal interphalangeal (DIP) crease and the liquid should be injected slowly. Enough liquid should be injected into the finger to fill out the wrinkles and round out the friction ridge skin so the shape is as similar as possible to a living finger (Figure 4.10). Once the desired shape is achieved, the needle should be slowly removed and the finger tied with string or a ziptie above the injection site; it is best to tie the

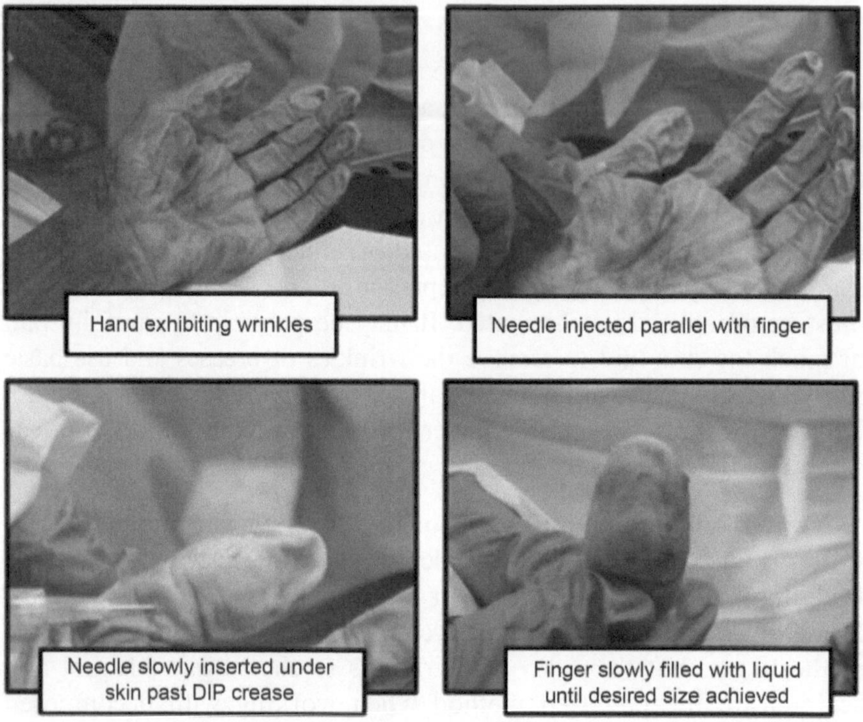

Figure 4.10 Steps in the Injection Technique (©NYC OCME 2012).

string or ziptie around the distal interphalangeal crease. Once there is visible and unobstructed friction ridge detail, it can be recorded using one of the basic fingerprint recovery techniques.

Injection Technique Supplies
Water, saline solution, isopropyl (rubbing) alcohol, acetone, Dermafil®, Dodge Metaflow®, tissue builder, or glycerin
String or Zipties
Syringe
Needle
Scissors

4.4 DEGLOVING TECHNIQUE

Note: Depending on the jurisdiction, there may be restrictions on removing the decedent's tissue and advanced approval may be required from the medical examiner.

During postmortem changes, various biological factors involved in decomposition affect the condition of the epidermis. The Degloving Technique is an advanced fingerprint recovery technique used when working with a decedent exhibiting decomposition and putrefaction, in which the friction ridge skin is significantly fragile, rubbery, and is separating from the underlying tissues. The fingerprint technician must exercise extreme care when handling degloving skin, as it can easily tear and destroy the friction ridge information that cannot be recovered. The visible ridge detail should be photographed prior to using this technique, which may further deteriorate the friction skin.

When assessing the friction ridge skin, if the skin is still partially attached to the underlying tissue, it may be possible to carefully pull the skin taut and use basic recovery techniques with extreme care. If the skin slippage is occurring in most areas, but there is adherence in a few areas, the skin can be carefully pinched in those areas and should easily come apart from the underlying tissue. If the skin is too fragile, or severe skin slippage is occurring, the friction ridge skin should be carefully removed from the underlying tissue as soon as possible. Before removing the skin, it is important to have paper towels or tech wipes set up and marked with each finger, as well as labeled containers for each portion of skin removed from respective fingers.

If degloving skin is very loose, it should come off easily by simply pulling the entire epidermal layer off like a glove (Figure 4.11a). Another method is to carefully twist the loose skin off of the finger (Figure 4.11b). If portions of the epidermal skin containing friction ridge detail have lifted off of the dermis, but some portion is still attached to the hand, small curved scissors and forceps can be used to carefully cut around the friction ridge detail (Figure 4.11c). The skin should be removed one finger at a time to avoid confusion.

After the skin is removed, it is rinsed with warm water and placed in a small container filled with some isopropyl (rubbing) alcohol, which is then sealed and slowly inverted a few times. This will clean and remove any excess moisture from the skin. The skin is removed with forceps and must be thoroughly dried by placing it between paper towels or tech wipes. If decomposition is advanced, there may be no discernable friction ridge detail available on the epidermis. If the

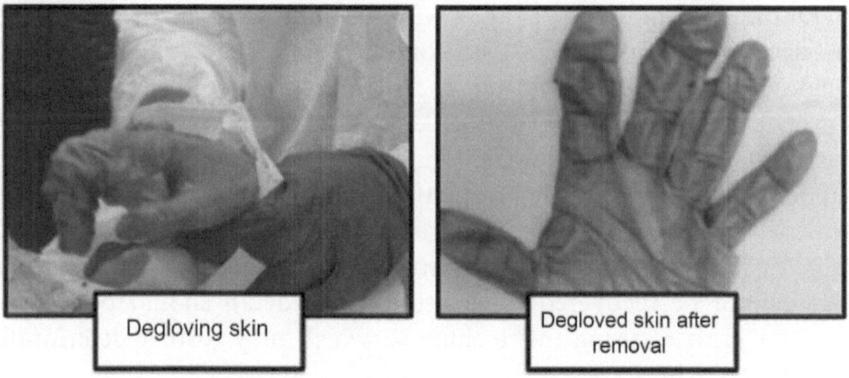

Figure 4.11a Degloving skin before and after removal (©NYC OCME 2012).

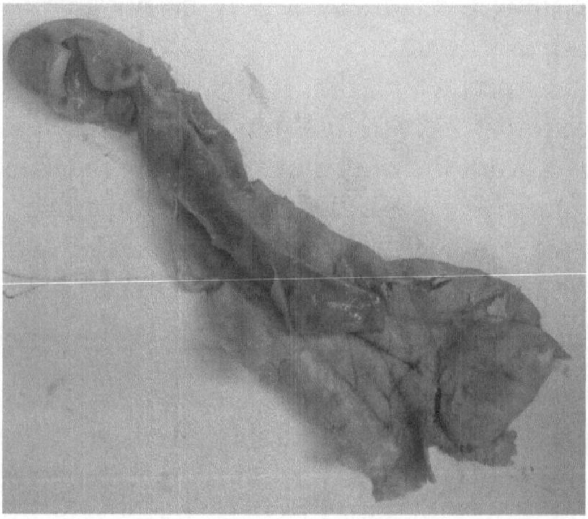

Figure 4.11b Degloving skin twisted off the finger (©NYC OCME 2012).

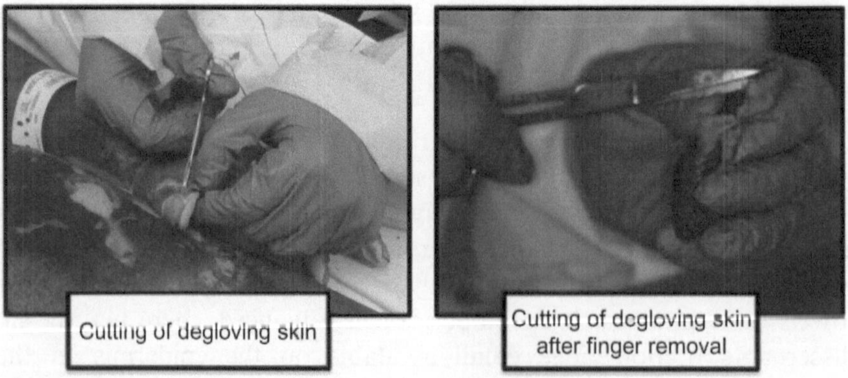

Figure 4.11c Degloving skin carefully cut off the finger (©NYC OCME 2012).

epidermis is destroyed, its underside can be used to record fingerprint impressions. The fingerprint impressions will be tonally reversed (white ridges) and the position of ridge flow will also be reversed. The reversal can be corrected by photography coupled with a graphics-editing program such as Adobe Photoshop®.

Once the skin is dry and there is visible friction ridge detail, it can be placed over the fingerprint technician's gloved finger and recorded using one of the basic fingerprint recovery techniques (Figure 4.12). If the skin is a partial portion of the friction ridge skin or ripped, another method is to flatten the skin over a piece of duct seal or plumbers putty and recorded using the powder/acetate/adhesive lifter technique. If the skin is too fragile to attempt the aforementioned methods, it can be trimmed using small curved scissors, placed in between two pieces of glass, and photographed. Another method is to use transmitted lighting by photographing the skin on a portable X-ray film

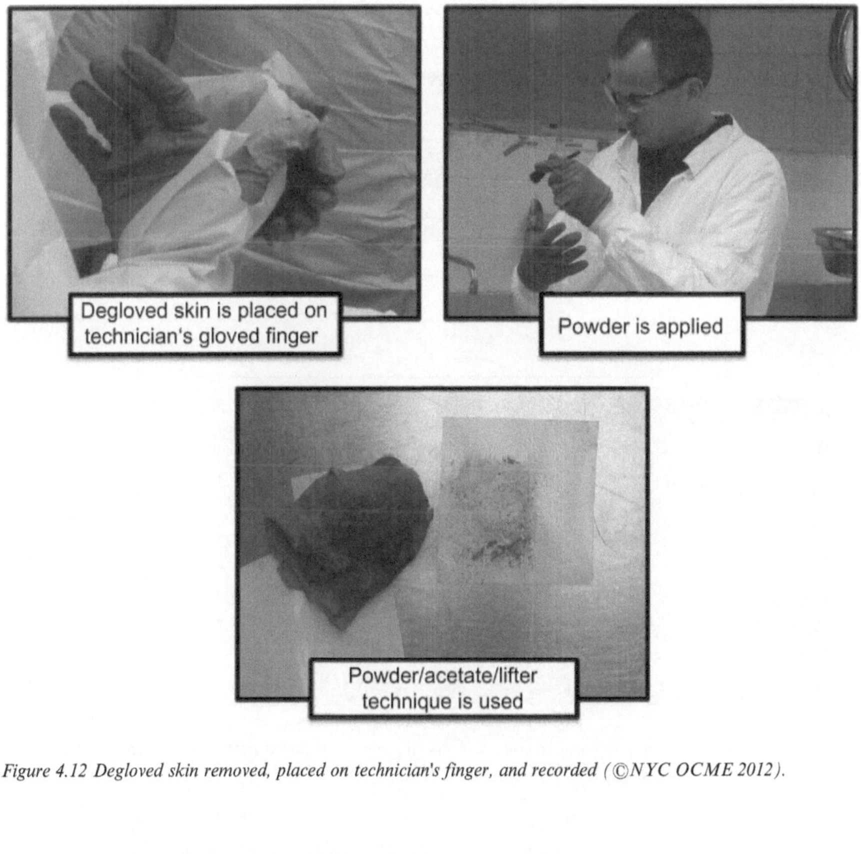

Figure 4.12 Degloved skin removed, placed on technician's finger, and recorded (©NYC OCME 2012).

illuminator viewer which has been placed on a copy stand containing a DSLR camera with macro lens and external flash (Figure 4.13). The skin can also be placed on a black background and photographed under a dissection microscope, coupled with oblique lighting (Figure 4.14a). If this method does not work, the skin can be dusted lightly with black powder and placed on a white background, then photographed under a dissection microscope, coupled with oblique lighting (Figure 4.14b). Once the fingerprint impression is recorded from the skin, it should be placed in the respective labeled container and returned back with the remains.

Figure 4.13 Degloved skin photographed on portable x-ray film illuminator viewer (©NYC OCME 2012).

Figure 4.14a,b Degloved skin photographed on black background, then dusted with black fingerprint powder and photographed on white background (©NYC OCME 2012).

Degloving Technique Supplies
All supplies from Powder/Acetate/Lifter Technique
Small curved scissors
Small forceps
Small containers, such as urine specimen cups or conical tubes
Photomacrographic scale
Digital single lens reflex (DSLR) camera with macro lens, external flash, and copystand or dissection microscope with digital camera attachment
Dual gooseneck lighting
Portable x-ray film illuminator viewer

4.5 BOILING TECHNIQUE

In some cases of advanced decomposition, friction ridge detail may not be detected because the top layers of friction ridge skin may already be completely destroyed. In these instances, the layer of the friction ridge skin underneath the epidermis, known as the dermis, may reveal discernible friction ridge detail and can be recorded or photographed successfully. The Boiling Technique is an advanced fingerprint recovery technique used when working with a decedent exhibiting severe decomposition and putrefaction, in which the epidermal layer of friction ridge skin has been destroyed and only the dermal layer remains. The fingerprint technician may at first see little or no discernible friction ridge detail and must exercise significant care when handling dermal skin, as it is the last layer of friction ridge information left that cannot be recovered if it is destroyed (Figure 4.15).

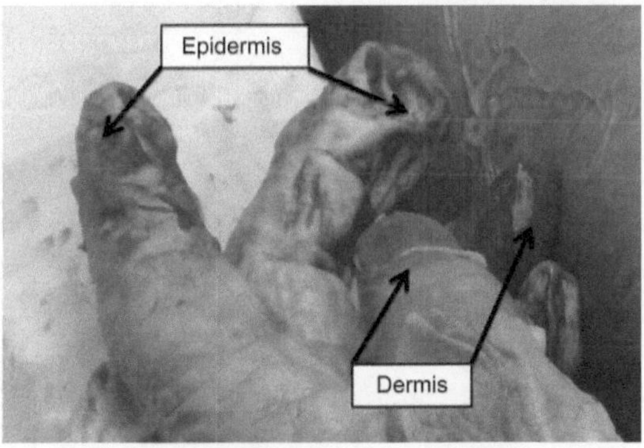

Figure 4.15 Degloving epidermal skin and exposed dermal skin (©NYC OCME 2012).

Any visible ridge detail should be photographed prior to using this technique, which may further deteriorate the friction skin.

The recorded dermal fingerprint impressions will appear differently than epidermal fingerprint impressions because the dermal impression will exhibit a double fine line created by the dermal papillae. When compared to the epidermal impression, each double row of dermal papillae represents a single epidermal ridge (Figure 4.16). There are also instances when the epidermis is only partially sloughing off and parts of the dermis are exposed. The dermal ridge appears as a double fine line wherever it meets the single fine line of the epidermal ridge (Figure 4.17).

Figure 4.16 Epidermal friction ridge detail and dermal friction ridge detail. (Reprinted from Uhle & Leas, 2007)

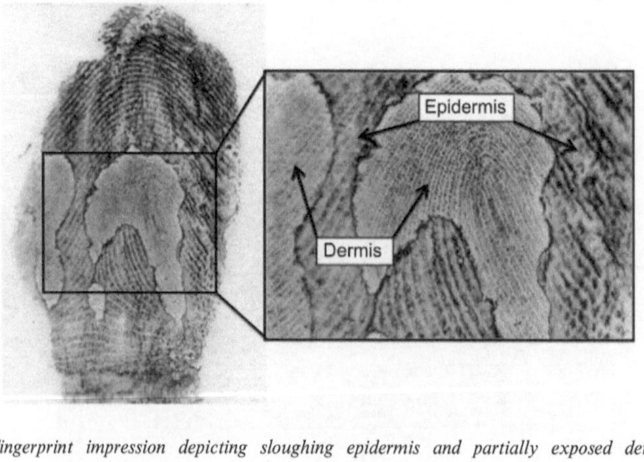

Figure 4.17 Fingerprint impression depicting sloughing epidermis and partially exposed dermis (©NYC OCME 2013).

In a 2013 analysis of 172 postmortem fingerprint cases requiring fingerprint acquisition at the New York City Office of Chief Medical Examiner, 73% of all cases required the use of epidermal impression, 10% required the use of dermal impressions, and 17% required the use of both epidermal and dermal impressions (Mulawka et al. 2013). These statistics support the importance of using both skin layers when acquiring post-mortem fingerprint impressions (Figure 4.18).

Fingerprints from the dermis can be recovered by using the Boiling Technique, a method that involves the use of boiling water to enhance ridge detail in the dermal skin through the process of osmotic rehydration (Uhle & Leas, 2007). The hands will be soft, pliable, and the ridges of the dermis will appear flat (Figure 4.19). Water is brought to a boil just below boiling point and maintained at this temperature in an electric hot water kettle or metal pot coupled with a hotplate.

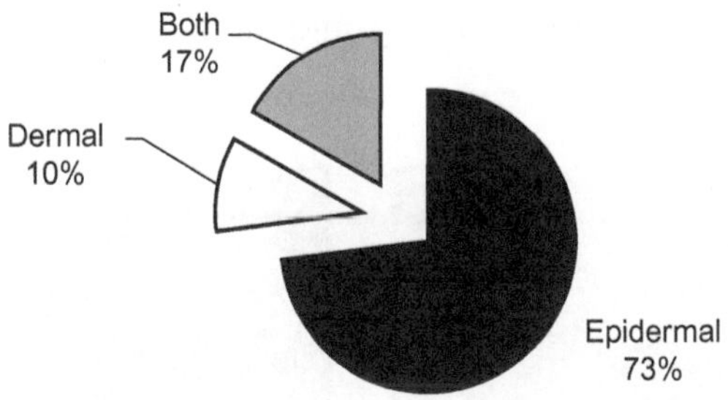

Figure 4.18 Use and frequency of epidermal and dermal fingerprint impressions on 172 Cases at the NYC OCME (Mulawka, Mosco, Uhle & Mokleby, 2013).

Figure 4.19 Macerated hand prior to boiling (left) and hand exhibiting dermal skin after boiling (right) (Reprinted from Uhle & Leas, 2007).

The container with boiling water is unplugged or taken off the heat source and the decedent's hand or fingers are carefully submerged in the hot water for five to ten seconds. It is best to lower the friction ridge being processed into the hot water source, as opposed to moving the hot water source, as this may be dangerous and cause the hot water to spill. The hand should slowly be removed from the water and inspected for dermal friction ridge detail, which will be visible if the hot water has plumped the dermal skin. If no discernible ridge detail is visualized, the hand should be placed back into the water for another five to ten seconds. A shorter time may be needed when severe decomposition or fine ridge detail is present. A longer time may be necessary during other circumstances; the process should be repeated for no more than thirty seconds total (Figure 4.20). In the event the friction ridge detail contains any sort of trauma, such as defects or abrasions, hot water application should be avoided in these areas, as they will be enhanced by the hot water as well. An alternative method is to indirectly apply the hot water to any undamaged areas of friction ridge

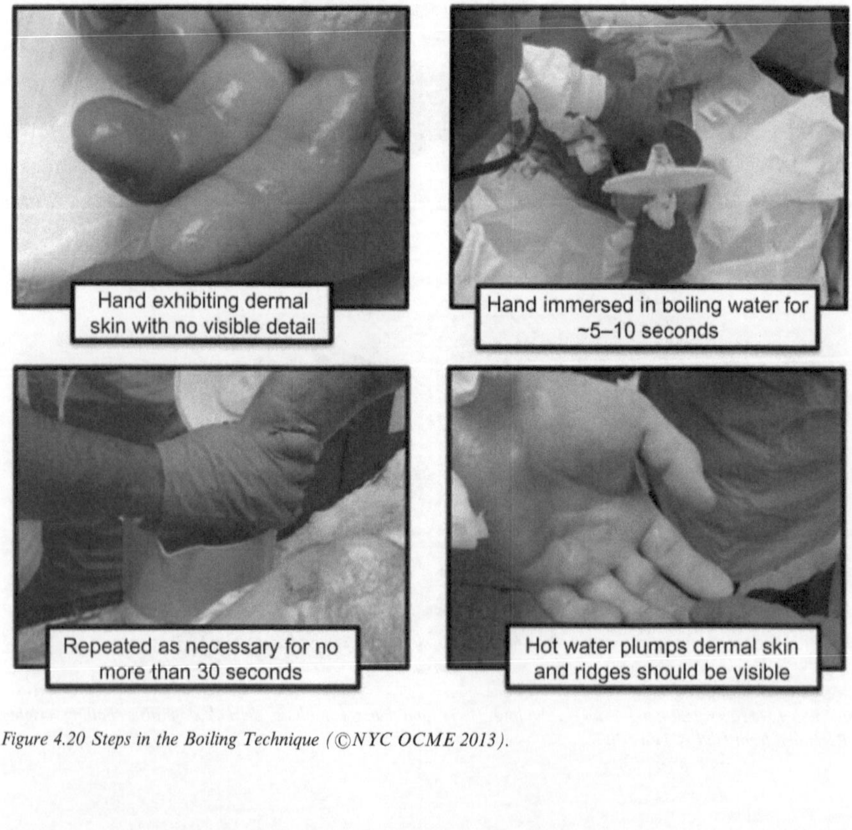

Figure 4.20 Steps in the Boiling Technique (©NYC OCME 2013).

skin. A sponge or foam paintbrush can be used to apply the hot water and avoid any defects that may obscure reconditioned ridge detail.

Once the dermal ridge detail is enhanced, the raised detail is carefully cleaned with tech wipes, paper towels, or a soft-bristled toothbrush and warm water. The skin should be brushed in the direction of ridge flow. The skin is then blotted dry with isopropyl alcohol and paper towels or by using a blow dryer on the warm setting. Once the skin is dry and there is visible friction ridge detail, it can be recorded using one of the basic fingerprint recovery techniques. The recorded dermal fingerprint impressions will exhibit significantly more ridge detail after using the Boiling Technique (Figure 4.21).

The examination and potential fingerprint recovery of burned or charred remains can also be a difficult task. The friction ridge skin may appear brittle, dry, and is very delicate. The fingerprint technician must exercise extreme care when handling charred skin, as it can easily fall apart and destroy the friction ridge information in such a way that it cannot be recovered. Any visible ridge detail should be photographed prior to using this technique, which may further deteriorate the friction skin.

If the skin is extremely fragile, the friction ridge skin should be carefully removed from the underlying tissue as soon as possible. Before removing the skin, it is important to have paper towels or tech wipes set up and marked with each finger, as well as labeled containers for each portion of skin removed from respective fingers. If the charred skin is hardened or very loose, it should be carefully twisted off of the

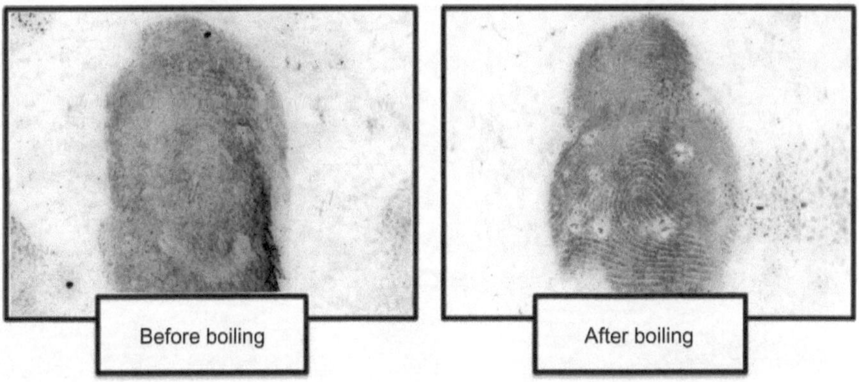

Figure 4.21 Dermal fingerprint impressions before and after use of the Boiling Technique (©NYC OCME 2013).

finger. If portions of the epidermal skin containing friction ridge detail have lifted off of the dermis, but some portion is still attached to the hand, small curved scissors and forceps can be used to carefully cut around the friction ridge detail and removed. The skin should be removed one finger at a time to avoid confusion.

If the epidermal layer of skin is destroyed, the dermal layer may still contain discernible ridge detail and the Boiling Technique should be used, followed by recording using one of the basic fingerprint recovery techniques. When a human body is burned, the body exhibits a pugilistic position and the hands become clenched into fists (Figure 4.22a-b). This can preserve the friction ridge detail on the fingers. It may be necessary to remove the fingers to access the friction ridge detail.

Boiling Technique Supplies
All supplies from Basic Fingerprint Recovery Techniques
Electric hot water kettle or metal pot and hotplate
Extension cord
Soft-bristled toothbrush
Digital single lens reflex (DSLR) camera with macro lens and external flash
Photomacrographic scale
Sponge or foam paint brush (optional)
Blow dryer (optional)

4.6 REHYDRATION TECHNIQUE

Note: Depending on the jurisdiction, there may be restrictions on removing the decedent's fingers and advanced approval may be required from the medical examiner.

(a) (b)

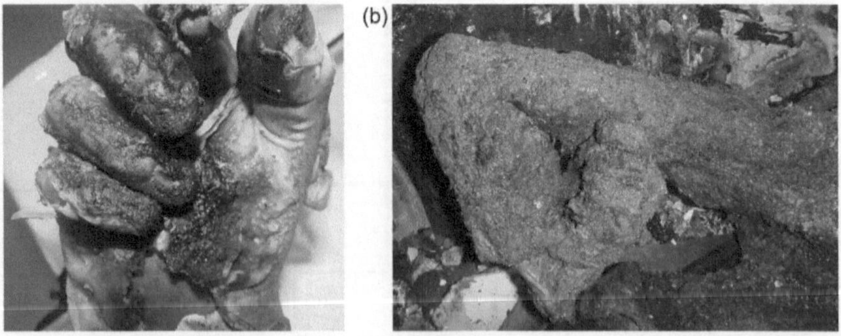

Figure 4.22a–b Clenched fists of burn victims (©NYC OCME 2013).

When desiccation or charring of the remains occurs, the friction ridge skin is dehydrated and the tissue shrinks, resulting in wrinkled and very tough skin (Figure 4.23). This severe damage of the friction ridge skin is the most difficult and time-consuming to recondition. Often, the body also exhibits rigor mortis, which results in clenched fists and difficulty accessing the friction ridge detail. When this occurs and rigor mortis cannot be overcome by forcefully straightening the fingers, the fingers may need to be removed from the hand in order to access and recondition the friction ridges.

Before removing the fingers, it is important to have paper towels or tech wipes set up and marked with each finger, as well as labeled containers for each of the respective fingers that will be amputated. Amputation of desiccated fingers is best achieved by using 27-inch loppers, which have a 2-inch cutting capacity. The fingers should be removed one at a time to avoid confusion. The lopper blades should be positioned over the proximal phalange, just above the knuckle area. If the lopper blades do not amputate the finger easily, scissors or a scalpel can be used to cut through any remaining tissue in order to completely separate the finger from the hand. The fingers can be transferred into their respectively labeled containers as they are removed.

The fingerprint technician should assess each amputated finger; this can be achieved by taking each finger out of its container with forceps and placing it under a magnifying glass to look for friction ridges. After examination of the amputated fingers, if visible ridge detail is present, photographs should be taken prior to using the Rehydration Technique, which may further deteriorate or destroy the friction skin

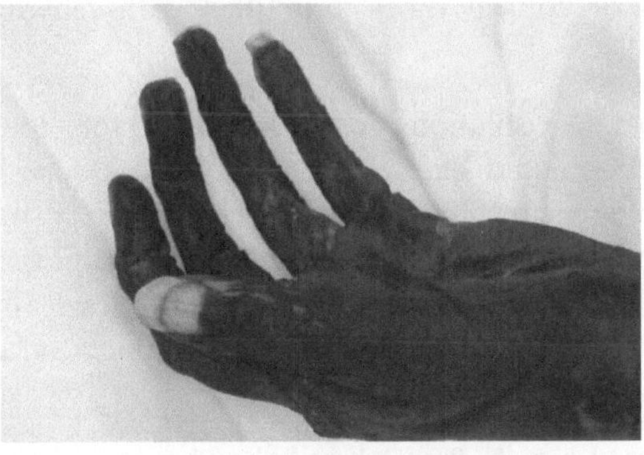

Figure 4.23 Hand exhibiting desiccated fingers (©NYC OCME 2013).

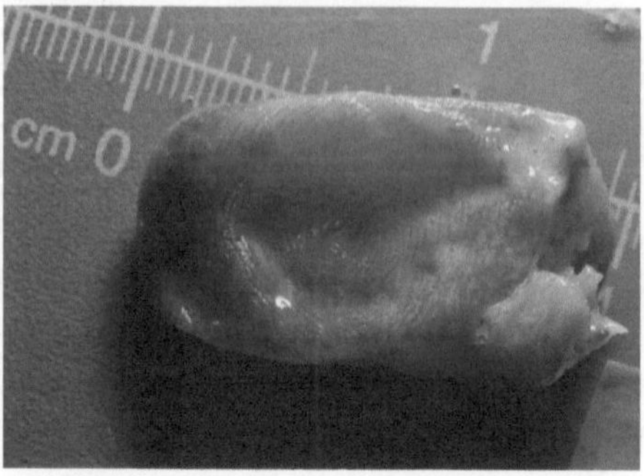

Figure 4.24 Photograph of finger prior to Rehydration Technique (©NYC OCME 2013).

Figure 4.25 Fingers in containers for Rehydration Technique (©FBI 2013).

(Figure 4.24). Additionally, the Casting Technique may be attempted at the examiner's discretion. If the Casting Technique is not successful, the fingers can be placed into labeled sealable containers, such as urine specimen cups or conical tubes and filled with rehydration solution (Figure 4.25).

Various soaking solutions can be used for the Rehydration Technique, such as liquid soap[1], bath wash[2], and Dodge Metaflow®. In addition, different chemical methods for rehydrating postmortem friction ridge skin have been published, such as soaking the fingers in 1% to 3% sodium or potassium hydroxide (FBI, 1979) or in the leather conditioner Lexol® (Uhle, 2010). Additionally, the bromine injection method,

[1]The authors have found Palmolive® liquid soap to be most effective.

[2]The author has found Johnson's® Baby Bedtime Bath wash to be most effective; special thanks to Lisa Mokleby and Dennis Percopo for developing this technique.

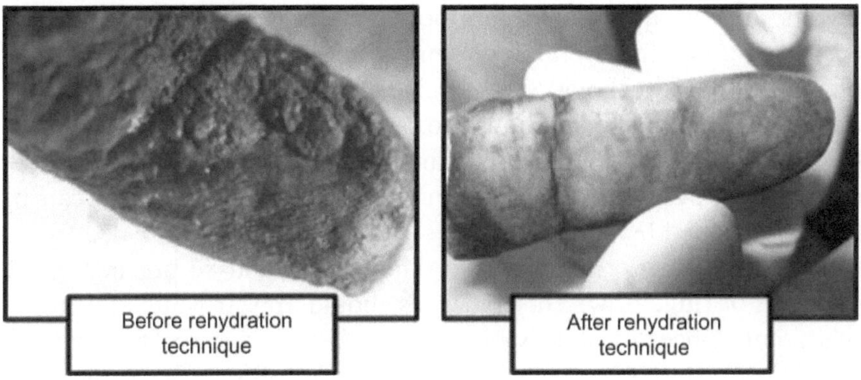

Figure 4.26 Finger before and after Rehydration Technique using alcohol and bromine (Reprinted from Mulawka, 2008).

employed by the Los Angeles County Coroner's Office, uses various concentrations of bromine and alcohol injected under the skin to rehydrate epidermal friction ridge skin, resulting in the successful creation of legible fingerprints (Figure 4.26) (Mulawka, 2008). The San Diego County Medical Examiner's Office uses a 50/50 solution of Dodge Metaflow® and Dodge Restorative® embalming fluids (Mulawka, 2008). Another rehydration method is the Ruffner Rehydration technique, which uses a mixture of sodium carbonate, ethanol, and water to rehydrate the postmortem desiccated fingers (Schmidt, et al. 2000).

Many of these chemical techniques are labor intensive and require the use of uncommon and costly materials, including chemicals and detergents that may destroy tissues. As such, the author's preferred method is to use liquid soap or bath wash for rehydration solutions, because both are very cost-effective and the least labor-intensive rehydration methods. The bath wash has been found to be the most effective and most rapid rehydration method because it serves as a detergent and moisturizer for the skin.

The liquid soap or bath wash can be diluted with warm water. Each container should be filled with enough solution to cover the ridge detail completely. The containers are sealed and stored in a secure location at room temperature for at least 24 hours. Finger rehydration may take hours or days due to the unique circumstances of each case and extent of desiccation. As there is no set time frame for when the skin will become pliable, the fingerprint examiner must regularly check the fingers for skin pliability, preferably daily. If the fingers are left in solution for too long, the friction ridge may be destroyed and unrecoverable. When checking the fingers to determine pliability, the skin should start to give slightly under pressure when it is ready. Some of the solutions are potentially destructive to the friction ridge skin and may cause some shedding of the epidermal layer of friction ridge skin. Since the outer layers may shed, they can be further removed by gently brushing the skin with a soft-bristled toothbrush under warm running water. The skin should be brushed in the direction of ridge flow. The epidermis should appear white and soft at this point. Once the skin is pliable and there is visible friction ridge detail with no depressions, it can be recorded using one of the basic fingerprint recovery techniques (Figure 4.27a). If the skin exhibits depressions, the Putty or Casting Techniques should be attempted. If the aforementioned methods are unsuccessful but the skin remains pliable, the fingers may require the Injection Technique (Figure 4.27b). If the entire epidermal layer has sloughed off, the Boiling Technique may be necessary and the examiner must use discretion, as this may further deteriorate the already fragile friction ridge skin (Figure 4.27c). The finger can also be photographed under a dissection microscope, DSLR camera with macro lens or coupled with oblique lighting (Figure 4.27d). Once the fingerprint impression is recorded from the skin, it should be placed in the respective labeled container and returned back with the remains.

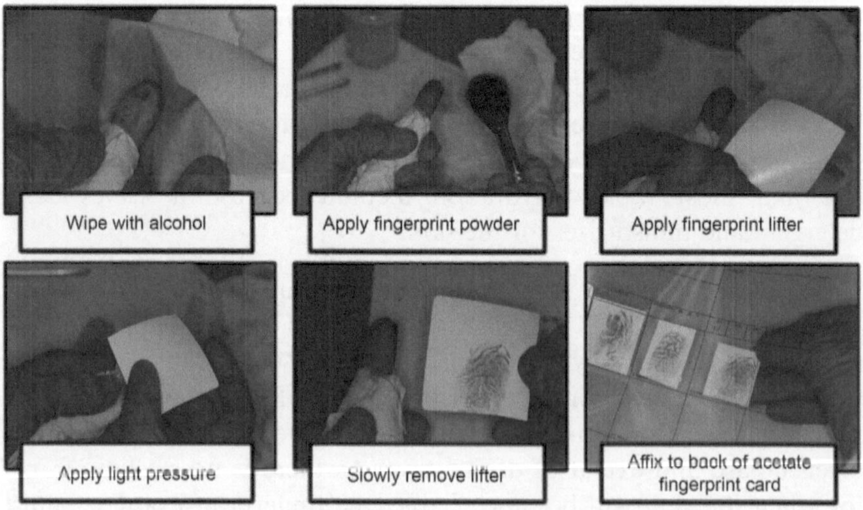

Figure 4.27a Powder/Acetate/Lifter Technique used on fingers after the Rehydration Technique (©NYC OCME 2012).

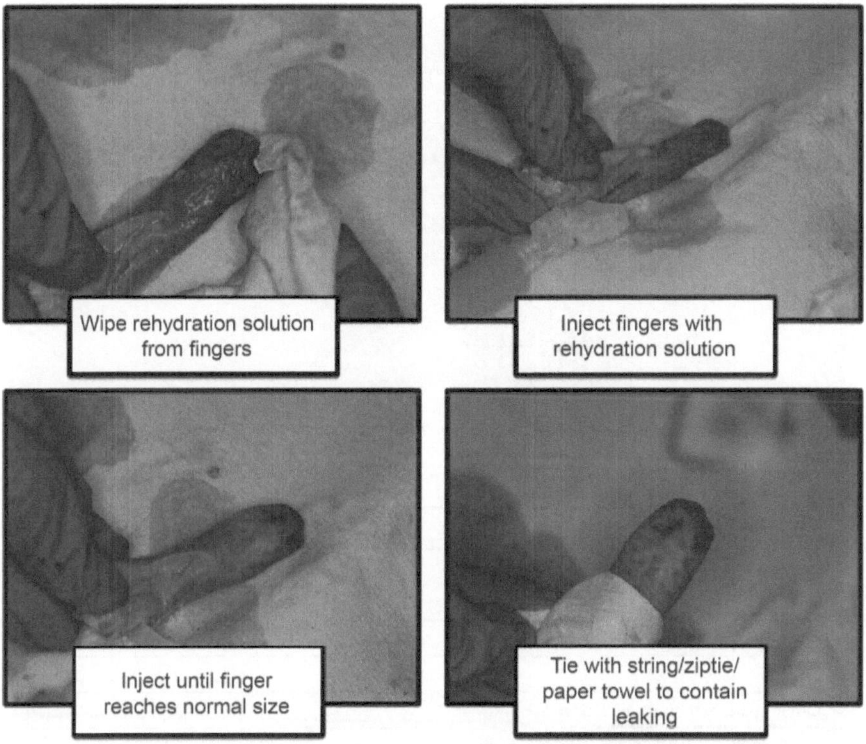

Figure 4.27b Injection Technique used on fingers after the Rehydration Technique (©NYC OCME 2012).

Figure 4.27c Boiling Technique used on fingers after the Rehydration Technique (©NYC OCME 2012).

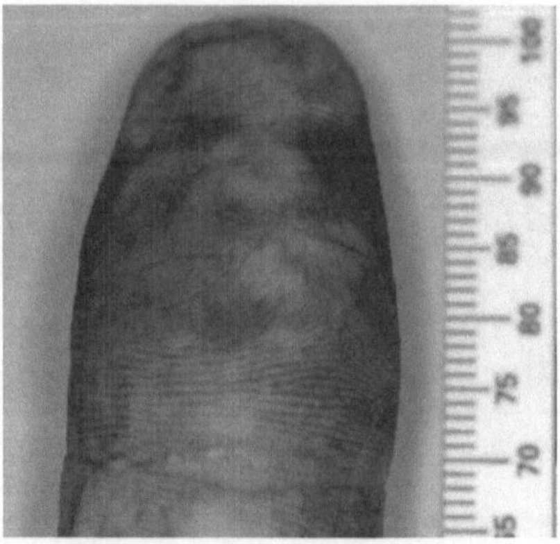

Figure 4.27d Photograph of finger after the Rehydration Technique (©NYC OCME 2012).

Rehydration Technique Supplies
Loppers
Scissors
Scalpel handle and blade
Forceps
Liquid soap, bath wash, or Dodge Metaflow®
Small containers, such as urine specimen cups or conical tubes
Magnifying glass
Soft-bristled toothbrush
All supplies from Powder/Acetate/Lifter Technique
All supplies from Putty Technique
All supplies from Casting Technique
All supplies from Injection Technique
Digital single lens reflex (DSLR) camera with macro lens, external flash, and copystand or dissection microscope with digital camera attachment
Dual gooseneck lighting

4.7 MOISTURIZER TECHNIQUE

If the friction ridge skin is dehydrated but remains pliable, the less-invasive Moisturizer Technique[3] can be used. This method involves application of a moisturizing bath wash to the friction ridge detail on the fingers. The solution should be massaged into the fingers and

[3]The author has found Johnson's® Baby Bedtime Bath wash to be most effective; special thanks to Lisa Mokleby and Dennis Percopo for developing this technique.

cover all of the ridge detail that will be used for recording. Sealable biohazard bags or sealable plastic bags are then placed over the hands and tied at the wrist using string, ziptics, or rubber bands. The hands should remain in the plastic for a few hours and checked periodically for pliability. The skin should start to give slightly under pressure when it is ready. Once the skin is pliable and there is visible friction ridge detail with no depressions, it can be recorded using one of the basic fingerprint recovery techniques. If the skin exhibits depressions, the Putty or Casting Techniques should be attempted. If the aforementioned methods are unsuccessful but the skin remains pliable, the fingers may require the Injection Technique. The finger can also be photographed using a DSLR camera with macro lens and external flash. The Moisturizer Technique has been found to be the most effective, rapid, least-invasive, and least-destructive rehydration method because it serves as a detergent and moisturizer for the skin.

Moisturizer Technique Supplies
Johnson's Baby Bedtime Bath®
Sealable biohazard bags or plastic bags
String, zipties, or rubberbands
Scissors
All supplies from Powder/Acetate/Lifter Technique
All supplies from Putty Technique
All supplies from Casting Technique
All supplies from Injection Technique
Digital single lens reflex (DSLR) camera with macro lens and external flash
Photomacrographic scale

CHAPTER 5

Manual and Digital Acquisition of Unidentified Postmortem Fingerprint Records

Postmortem fingerprints can be acquired utilizing two main methods—manual fingerprint acquisition using Basic or Advanced Postmortem Fingerprint Recovery techniques (described in detail in Chapters 3 and 4) on a standard fingerprint card, or digital fingerprint acquisition using a livescan capture device. Both methods require postmortem fingerprints to be recorded on a specifically formatted card designated by the FBI to allow for electronic searching. The FBI has created guides to help local, state, and federal agencies report standardized information that is accurate and complete. Submitting the correct required information enables the FBI to expedite processing of the postmortem fingerprint cards and associated documents more promptly and with less chance of error. Missing, illegible, or incomplete data, as well as poor-quality fingerprint images, can lead to rejections and delays in processing. The FBI has also developed resources to assist local, state, and federal agencies in the preparation of the standardized fingerprint cards and in obtaining legible fingerprints. As there is no specific standard for postmortem fingerprint record acquisition, examples and instructions are delineated in this chapter that can help identify the correct manner by which postmortem data should be recorded on the fingerprint cards.

5.1 MANUAL POSTMORTEM FINGERPRINT ACQUISITION

The acquisition of postmortem fingerprint records can be achieved by using the Basic and Advanced Postmortem Fingerprint Recovery techniques described in detail in Chapters 3 and 4. Fingerprints are recorded manually on stock fingerprint cards or acetate sheets that have fingerprint cards photocopied or printed onto them. A specific type of standardized fingerprint card must be used to record

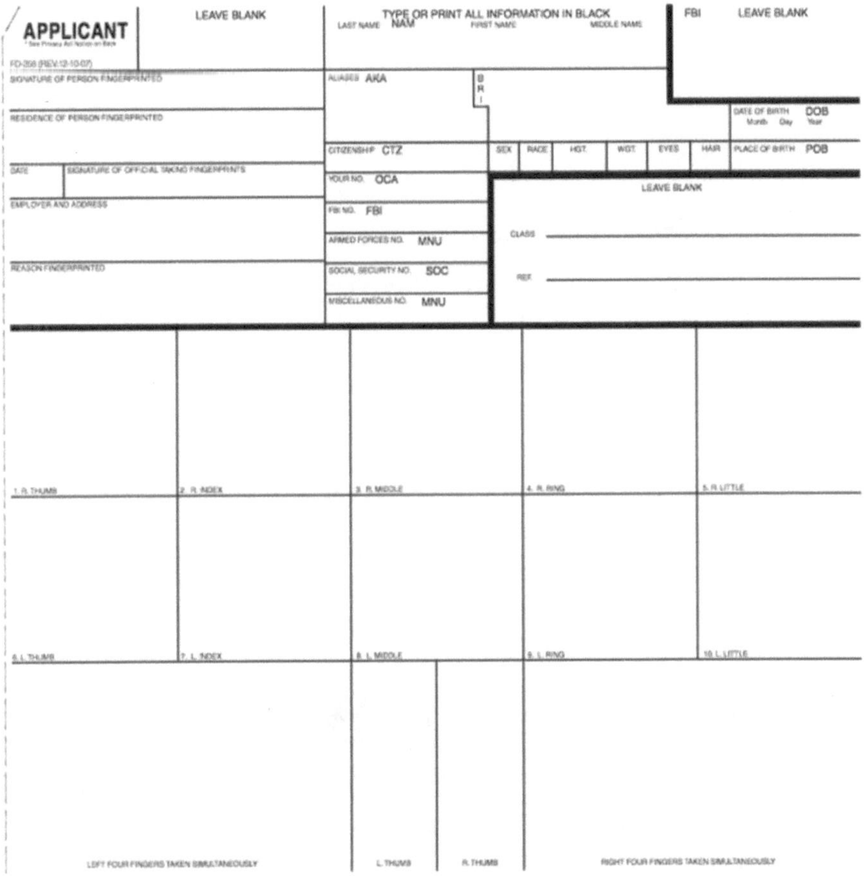
APPLICANT
LEAVE BLANK
TYPE OR PRINT ALL INFORMATION IN BLACK
LAST NAME NAM FIRST NAME MIDDLE NAME
FBI LEAVE BLANK
FD-258 (REV.12-10-07)
SIGNATURE OF PERSON FINGERPRINTED
ALIASES AKA
RESIDENCE OF PERSON FINGERPRINTED
DATE OF BIRTH DOB Month Day Year
CITIZENSHIP CTZ
SEX RACE HGT. WGT. EYES HAIR PLACE OF BIRTH POB
DATE SIGNATURE OF OFFICIAL TAKING FINGERPRINTS
YOUR NO. OCA
LEAVE BLANK
EMPLOYER AND ADDRESS
FBI NO. FBI
ARMED FORCES NO. MNU
CLASS
REASON FINGERPRINTED
SOCIAL SECURITY NO. SOC
REF.
MISCELLANEOUS NO. MNU
1. R. THUMB 2. R. INDEX 3. R. MIDDLE 4. R. RING 5. R. LITTLE
6. L. THUMB 7. L. INDEX 8. L. MIDDLE 9. L. RING 10. L. LITTLE
LEFT FOUR FINGERS TAKEN SIMULTANEOUSLY L. THUMB R. THUMB RIGHT FOUR FINGERS TAKEN SIMULTANEOUSLY

Figure 5.1a Standardized FBI Applicant Fingerprint Card (FD-258) (©FBI, 2007).

postmortem fingerprints for acceptable ten-print searching with the FBI according to the FBI's Guidelines for Preparation of Fingerprints and Associated Criminal History Information (2013). The FBI accepts two types of standardized fingerprints cards—the Applicant Fingerprint Card (FD-258, Figure 5.1a) and the Criminal Fingerprint Card (FD-249, Figure 5.1b). Currently, a specific standardized fingerprint card for postmortem fingerprint records submissions is not available and the Criminal Fingerprint Card must be used.

When a postmortem fingerprint record is acquired manually, it is important to include certain information on the fingerprint card. There

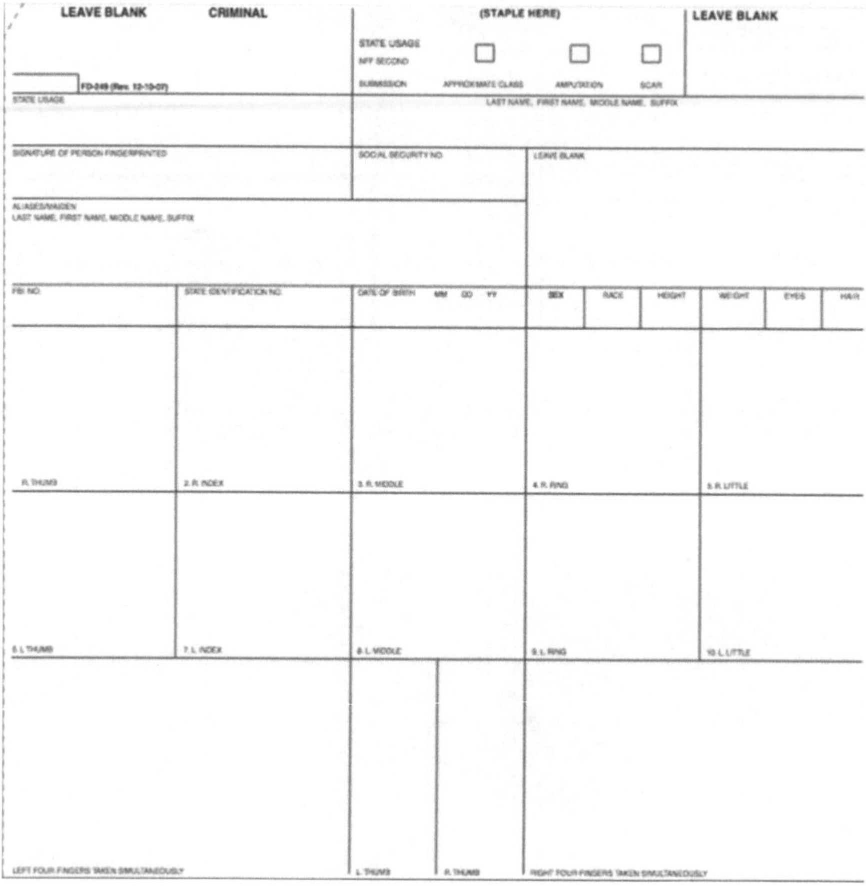
LEAVE BLANK
CRIMINAL
(STAPLE HERE)
LEAVE BLANK
STATE USAGE
NFF SECOND
SUBMISSION
APPROXIMATE CLASS
AMPUTATION
SCAR
FD-249 (Rev. 12-10-07)
STATE USAGE
LAST NAME, FIRST NAME, MIDDLE NAME, SUFFIX
SIGNATURE OF PERSON FINGERPRINTED
SOCIAL SECURITY NO.
LEAVE BLANK
ALIASES/MAIDEN
LAST NAME, FIRST NAME, MIDDLE NAME, SUFFIX
FBI NO.
STATE IDENTIFICATION NO.
DATE OF BIRTH MM DD YY
SEX
RACE
HEIGHT
WEIGHT
EYES
HAIR
R. THUMB
2. R. INDEX
3. R. MIDDLE
4. R. RING
5. R. LITTLE
6. L. THUMB
7. L. INDEX
8. L. MIDDLE
9. L. RING
10. L. LITTLE
LEFT FOUR FINGERS TAKEN SIMULTANEOUSLY
L. THUMB
R. THUMB
RIGHT FOUR FINGERS TAKEN SIMULTANEOUSLY

Figure 5.1b Standardized FBI Criminal Fingerprint Card (FD-249) (©FBI, 2007).

are five important pieces of information that should be recorded on the fingerprint card (Figure 5.2):

Information to Include on PM Fingerprint Card
1. Agency Case Number 2. "Unknown Deceased" in the name block 3. Name or initials of fingerprint technician(s) acquiring the fingerprints and date of acquisition 4. Gender of decedent (or unknown) 5. Techniques used at the bottom (optional) 6. "Deceased" written across slaps (optional)

Most agencies require the recording of slaps on a ten-print fingerprint card for sequence check purposes and reject the record if the slaps are missing. Generally, acquiring slaps will not be possible during postmortem

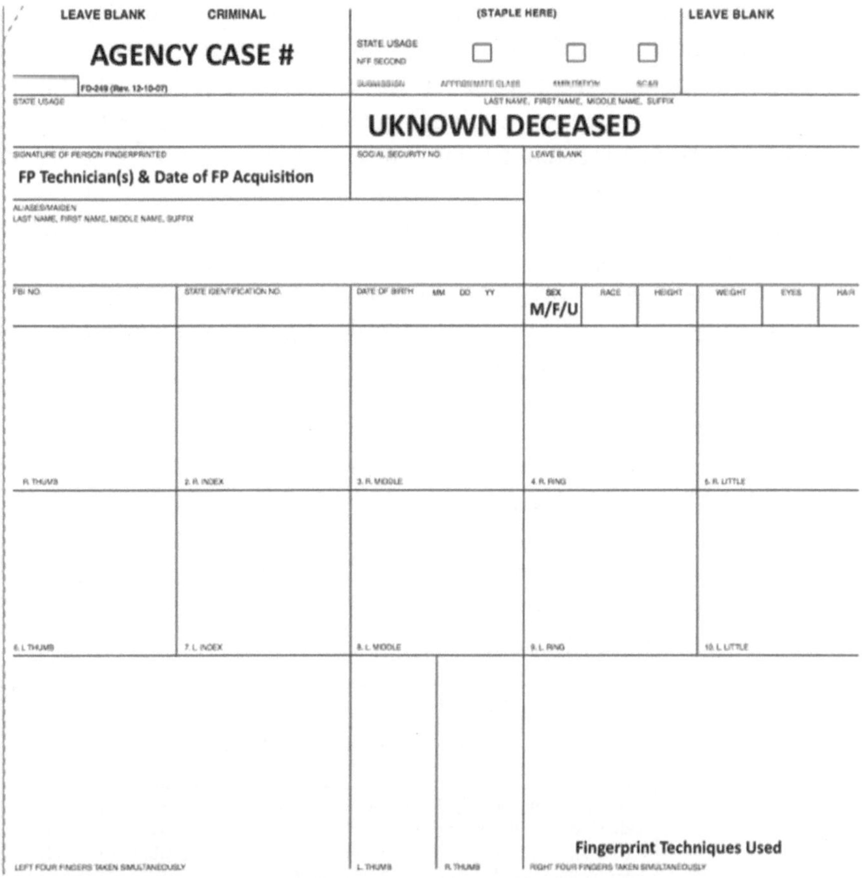
LEAVE BLANK CRIMINAL (STAPLE HERE) LEAVE BLANK
AGENCY CASE #
STATE USAGE
FD-249 (Rev. 12-10-07)
LAST NAME, FIRST NAME, MIDDLE NAME, SUFFIX
UKNOWN DECEASED
SIGNATURE OF PERSON FINGERPRINTED
FP Technician(s) & Date of FP Acquisition
SOCIAL SECURITY NO.
LEAVE BLANK
ALIASES/MAIDEN
LAST NAME, FIRST NAME, MIDDLE NAME, SUFFIX
FBI NO.
STATE IDENTIFICATION NO.
DATE OF BIRTH MM DD YY
SEX
M/F/U
RACE HEIGHT WEIGHT EYES HAIR
R. THUMB 2. R. INDEX 3. R. MIDDLE 4. R. RING 5. R. LITTLE
6. L THUMB 7. L INDEX 8. L MIDDLE 9. L RING 10. L LITTLE
LEFT FOUR FINGERS TAKEN SIMULTANEOUSLY
L. THUMB R. THUMB
Fingerprint Techniques Used
RIGHT FOUR FINGERS TAKEN SIMULTANEOUSLY

Figure 5.2 Important information to include on unidentified postmortem fingerprint record.

fingerprint recovery due to the condition of the remains and the presence of rigor mortis. In addition, the fingerprint impressions are often acquired from a decedent one at a time, so acquiring slaps one at a time would defeat the purpose of the slaps and might prove to be cumbersome. As such, the word "deceased" can be written across the slaps on the fingerprint card. However, this is optional, especially since multiple impressions can be taken of the same finger, placed in the slap impression area, and adequately labeled.

Nevertheless, it is very important to avoid including too much subjective information. For example, postmortem changes can lead to a significant change in skin color. As such, the fingerprint examiner should not record the decedent's race on the fingerprint card. Additionally, the unidentified decedent's age should not be included on the fingerprint card, as the estimate may prove to be inaccurate. Most importantly, if the decedent has a tentative name, the name should not be included on the postmortem fingerprint card. In the event the postmortem fingerprint record is identified to a different person, and the incorrect name is recorded on the postmortem fingerprint record, it can lead to confusion and increase the chances of an accidental misidentification. The tentative name can instead be included on the manual submission paperwork (Chapter 7) associated with the unidentified postmortem fingerprint record. It is important to remember that fingerprint identification is a scientific modality used in forensic human identification (Chapter 1) and subjective information must be kept to a minimum.

Another important aspect of manual postmortem fingerprint acquisition is to include any special techniques used that may affect the Automated Fingerprint Identification (AFIS) search, as the size of the fingerprint impression may be abnormal due to postmortem changes in the friction ridge skin (Chapter 7). There are different techniques used during postmortem fingerprint processing that should be documented for each finger on the card (Figure 5.3a–e):

Annotation	Reason
Not printable	If a finger is too damaged to recover any legible friction ridge detail from the dermis or epidermis.
Not printed	If a finger is significantly deteriorated and requires more advanced recovery techniques than the other fingers, the fingerprint technician may decide to not record the specific finger, especially if enough examination-quality friction ridge information is available from the other fingers.
Missing	The finger is missing.
Scar	The friction ridge detail exhibits an obvious antemortem scar.
Degloved	The corresponding antemortem fingerprint impression may be significantly smaller.
Injected	The corresponding antemortem fingerprint impression may be significantly smaller.
Dermal	The corresponding antemortem fingerprint impression may be significantly larger.
Burned/Charred	The corresponding antemortem fingerprint impression may be significantly larger.
Rehydrated	The corresponding antemortem fingerprint impression may be significantly larger.
Photo	An unaltered photograph of the finger is a positive impression of the corresponding antemortem fingerprint impression (which is a negative impression of the finger).
Casting	The casting of the finger is a three-dimensional impression of the corresponding two-dimensional antemortem fingerprint impression.
Latent submitted separately	If a specific finger requires more advanced techniques, including recording of a latent fingerprint impression, this will alert the examiner that friction ridge information is available and will be submitted separately from the ten-print record as a latent fingerprint impression.

(a)

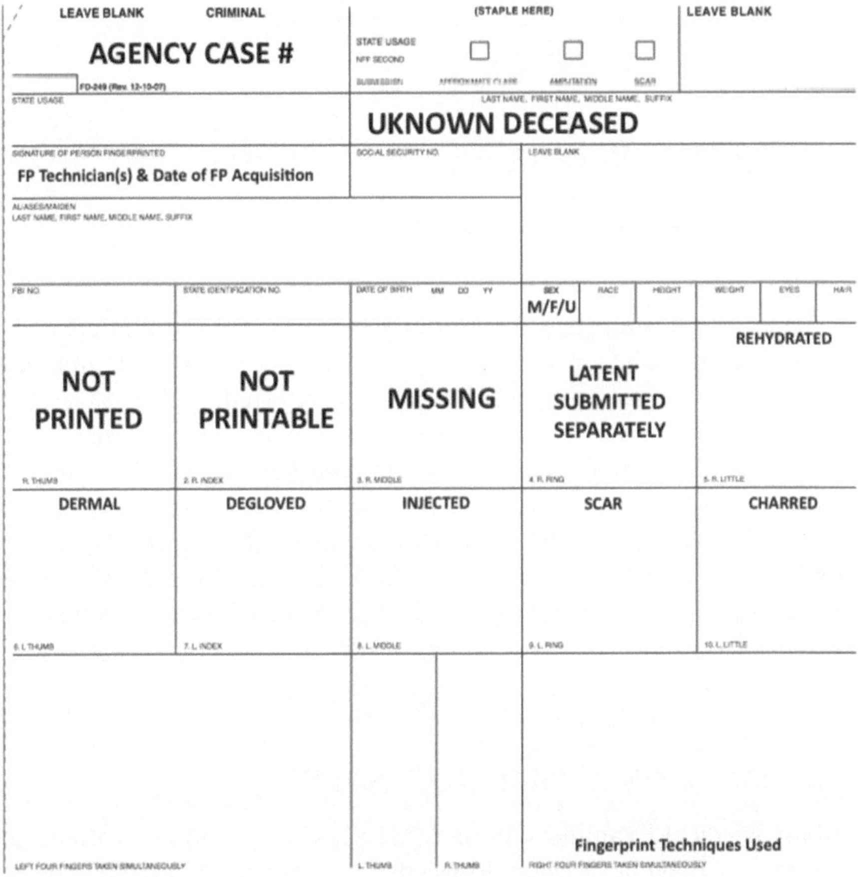

LEAVE BLANK | CRIMINAL | (STAPLE HERE) | LEAVE BLANK

AGENCY CASE #

FD-249 (Rev. 12-10-07)

STATE USAGE | NFF SECOND SUBMISSION | APPROXIMATE CLASS | AMPUTATION | SCAR

STATE USAGE

LAST NAME, FIRST NAME, MIDDLE NAME, SUFFIX

UKNOWN DECEASED

SIGNATURE OF PERSON FINGERPRINTED

FP Technician(s) & Date of FP Acquisition

SOCIAL SECURITY NO. | LEAVE BLANK

ALIASES/MAIDEN
LAST NAME, FIRST NAME, MIDDLE NAME, SUFFIX

FBI NO.	STATE IDENTIFICATION NO.	DATE OF BIRTH MM DD YY	SEX	RACE	HEIGHT	WEIGHT	EYES	HAIR
			M/F/U					

1. R. THUMB	2. R. INDEX	3. R. MIDDLE	4. R. RING	5. R. LITTLE
NOT PRINTED	NOT PRINTABLE	MISSING	LATENT SUBMITTED SEPARATELY	REHYDRATED

6. L. THUMB	7. L. INDEX	8. L. MIDDLE	9. L. RING	10. L. LITTLE
DERMAL	DEGLOVED	INJECTED	SCAR	CHARRED

LEFT FOUR FINGERS TAKEN SIMULTANEOUSLY | L. THUMB | R. THUMB | RIGHT FOUR FINGERS TAKEN SIMULTANEOUSLY

Fingerprint Techniques Used

Figure 5.3a Some of the important annotations and techniques to include on unidentified postmortem fingerprint record.

A separate internal document (paper or electronic form) should be utilized to record detailed information documenting any specific postmortem fingerprint recovery techniques used on each finger. Reconditioning techniques such as the Casting Technique, Rehydration Technique, Injection Technique, Degloving Technique, etc. should be recorded on this form for record-keeping purposes. The completed form should be saved with the physical or electronic case file and can be used as a reference when filling out the special techniques in manual submission paperwork (Chapter 7). The aforementioned annotations may not be available when capturing fingerprints using a digital livescan system due to strict requirements with the State Bureau and FBI (explained in next section).

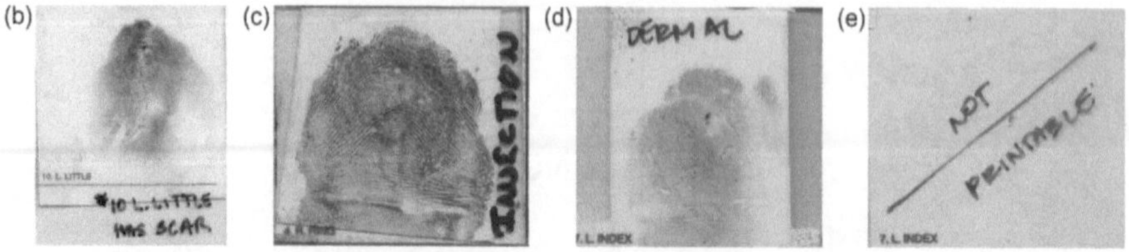

Figure 5.3b–e Examples of important annotations on postmortem fingerprint impressions.

Once the postmortem fingerprint record is filled out and created, it should be scanned on a high-resolution flatbed scanner at minimum 500 d.p.i. and saved in TIFF format (preferred, but JPEG, JPEG 2000, and PDF are also acceptable). Digital images acquired by this method are known as "off-line" images and the scanners used are typically not specifically designed for fingerprint applications (Moses, 2011). The digital fingerprint card is compatible with most programs and can be directly submitted to a local law enforcement agency and requested for AFIS searching, emailed as an attachment, and uploaded or saved into an electronic database with the corresponding case file (Chapter 7).

5.2 DIGITAL FINGERPRINT ACQUISITION

Many Medical Examiner/Coroner (ME/C) Offices and law enforcement agencies (LEAs) have begun to use digital livescan and cardscan devices to capture fingerprints from the deceased. Livescan and cardcan technology enables agencies tasked with forensic identification to electronically submit postmortem fingerprint records to the state and federal repositories, significantly reducing the time it takes to effect identifications. Livescan and cardscan images are known as on-line images. Although offline images are still in use in some agencies, online fingerprint images are increasingly being used and becoming the normal method of digital fingerprint acquisition in most agencies. Nevertheless, electronic fingerprint capture from the deceased and the living are significantly different. During electronic postmortem fingerprint acquisition, the recording platen is manipulated against the decedent (Figure 5.4a). Conversely, during electronic antemortem fingerprint acquisition, the live person is manipulated against the recording platen (Figure 5.4b). Current livescan devices were specifically designed for the living and were adopted for use with unidentified human remains.

The specific standardized criminal fingerprint card (FD-249, Figure 5.5) must also be used to electronically capture postmortem fingerprints for acceptable ten-print searching with the FBI according to the FBI's Guidelines for Preparation of Fingerprints and Associated Criminal History Information (2013). Additionally, specifications and requirements for submitting electronic fingerprint submissions are available in the FBI's Criminal Justice Information Services Electronic Biometric Transmission Specifications (EBTS) Manual (2013).

When a postmortem fingerprint record is acquired electronically, it is important to include certain information on the fingerprint card that is

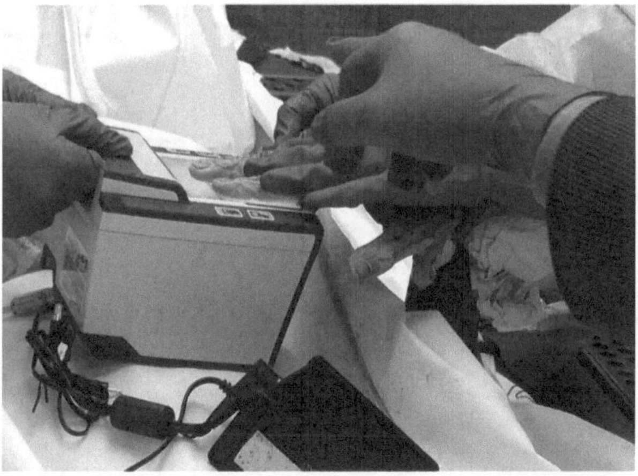

Figure 5.4a Postmortem electronic fingerprint capture from decedent with livescan device.

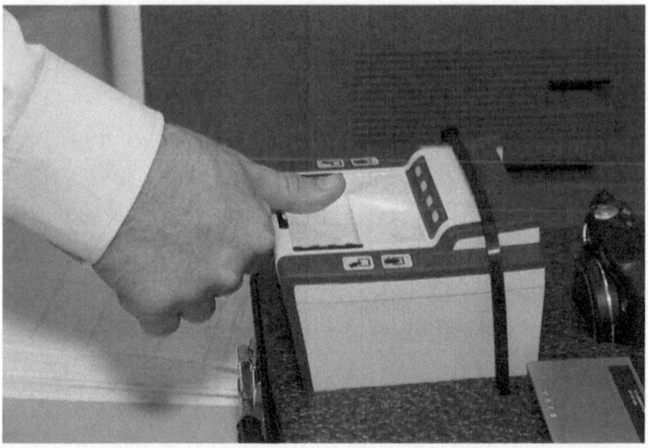

Figure 5.4b Antemortem electronic fingerprint capture from live person with livescan device.

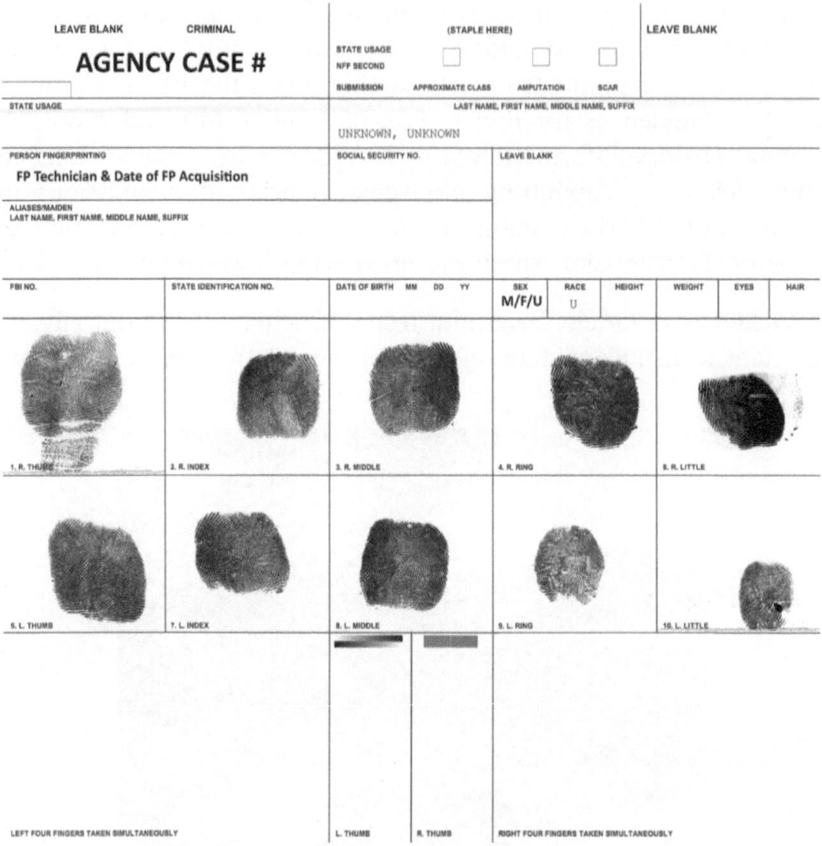

Figure 5.5 Example of electronic standardized FBI Criminal Fingerprint Card (FD-249) populated with postmortem fingerprints captured by a livescan device (©NYC OCME, 2013).

dictated by the state bureau requirements (the state bureau may have its own EBTS) and FBI CJIS EBTS. The ME/C office or LEA must work with the digital fingerprint acquisition vendor to meet these requirements. Additionally, most agencies require the capture of slaps on electronic ten-print submissions for sequence check purposes and reject the record if the slaps are missing. Generally, acquiring slaps will not be possible during electronic postmortem fingerprint recovery due to the condition of the remains and the presence of rigor mortis. Furthermore, the inclusion of any special techniques used that may affect the Automated Fingerprint Identification (AFIS) search is also dictated by the state and federal EBTS. Since AFIS technology was developed for the electronic searching of fingerprint impressions from the living and for criminal purposes, only certain annotations are allowed in the fingerprint blocks (amputated fingers, tip-amputated, transplanted fingers, missing at birth, deformed, bandaged, scars) and may not be applicable to postmortem fingerprint acquisition. Annotations applicable to postmortem fingerprint acquisition may be restricted and rejected by the state bureau and FBI. As such, the ME/C office or LEA must work with the digital fingerprint acquisition vendor, state, and FBI to meet all specified requirements.

One of the major challenges in acquiring digital fingerprints from the deceased has been recording legible fingerprints from desiccated, decomposed, and charred remains, or fingers exhibiting rigor mortis. The flat platen is difficult to manipulate around a decedent's fingers, as is capturing any friction ridge information located within depressions that have formed due to postmortem changes. Many of the current livescan devices are bulky and tethered to a computer, which further impedes efficient electronic fingerprint capture from the remains.

If the remains exhibit advanced postmortem changes, the fingers must be reconditioned before legible impressions can be captured electronically. This can be achieved by using the Advanced Postmortem Fingerprint Recovery Techniques described in detail in Chapter 4. The livescan device has the ability to capture postmortem dermal fingerprint impressions following the Boiling Technique. In addition, epidermal fingerprint impressions can be electronically captured using the Livescan following the Degloving or Injection Techniques. If the fingers need to be removed and rehydrated using the Rehydration Technique, electronic capture may also be possible once the friction ridge skin is enhanced. The Livescan device even has the ability to electronically capture the fingerprint impression generated when a casting is applied after using the Casting Technique; however, there is currently no way of searching casting impressions since they are captured in a different orientation than a regular electronic fingerprint impression (Figure 5.6).

In the event that fingerprints cannot be electronically acquired using the livescan device, even after reconditioning the fingers using Advanced Postmortem Fingerprint Recovery Techniques, the impressions should be recorded using manual techniques. The physical fingerprint card could be scanned using an FBI-approved cardscan high-resolution flatbed scanner (Figure 5.7a), which will scan the fingerprint record in an online electronic format that can then be electronically submitted to the state and federal repositories (Figure 5.7b). The digital

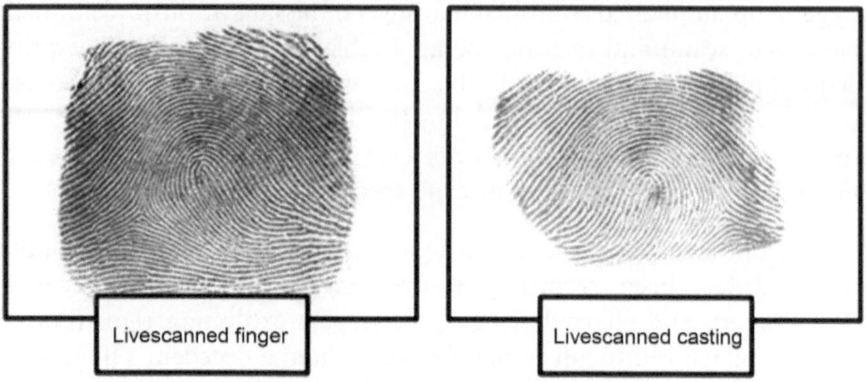

Figure 5.6 Regular electronic fingerprint impression and an electronic fingerprint impression captured of the finger's corresponding casting (©FBI, 2013).

Figure 5.7a FBI-approved cardscan device (©NYC OCME, 2013).

fingerprint information captured with livescan and cardscan devices is saved in a specific ANSI-NIST standard electronic format. The format is not compatible for allowing the images to be viewed without the livescan software, FBI Universal Latent Workstation (ULW) software,

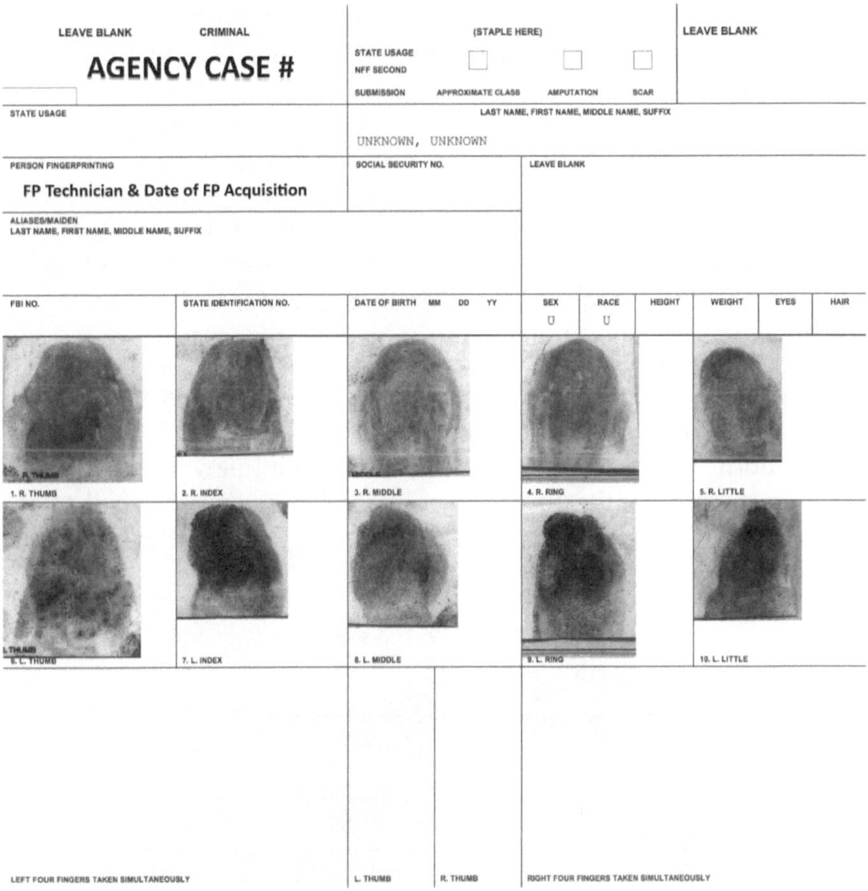
LEAVE BLANK CRIMINAL
AGENCY CASE #
(STAPLE HERE)
STATE USAGE
NFF SECOND
SUBMISSION APPROXIMATE CLASS AMPUTATION SCAR
LEAVE BLANK
STATE USAGE
LAST NAME, FIRST NAME, MIDDLE NAME, SUFFIX
UNKNOWN, UNKNOWN
PERSON FINGERPRINTING
FP Technician & Date of FP Acquisition
SOCIAL SECURITY NO.
LEAVE BLANK
ALIASES/MAIDEN
LAST NAME, FIRST NAME, MIDDLE NAME, SUFFIX

FBI NO.	STATE IDENTIFICATION NO.	DATE OF BIRTH MM DD YY	SEX	RACE	HEIGHT	WEIGHT	EYES	HAIR
			U	U				

1. R. THUMB
2. R. INDEX
3. R. MIDDLE
4. R. RING
5. R. LITTLE
6. L. THUMB
7. L. INDEX
8. L. MIDDLE
9. L. RING
10. L. LITTLE
LEFT FOUR FINGERS TAKEN SIMULTANEOUSLY
L. THUMB
R. THUMB
RIGHT FOUR FINGERS TAKEN SIMULTANEOUSLY

Figure 5.7b Example of electronic standardized FBI Criminal Fingerprint Card (FD-249) populated with postmortem fingerprints captured by a cardscan device (©NYC OCME, 2013).

or a specific NIST-viewing software program. The digital fingerprint file can be submitted electronically via a secure line connection to search through a local AFIS, state identification bureau, and eventually the FBI IAFIS/NGI. The file generated may be uploaded or saved into an electronic database with the corresponding case file.

5.3 CAPTURING EXAMINATION-QUALITY FINGERPRINTS

The condition of human remains declines as postmortem changes occur, resulting in deterioration of the friction ridge detail. Consequently, resulting fingerprint impressions are usually of worse quality than their antemortem standard. As such, postmortem fingerprint impressions must be acquired with maximum examination-quality in order to effectively search and subsequently identify postmortem fingerprint records (Figure 5.8). If a high-examination quality record is available for comparison but the post-mortem record is of too low quality, it can render the impressions of no value and prevent identification (Figure 5.9a,b). Legible fingerprint records are required for classification, comparison, and scanning into AFIS for searching. High examination-quality postmortem fingerprint acquisition is therefore crucial in order to maximize identification attempts of unidentified fingerprint records.

Additionally, the fingerprint technician should attempt to record as much legible detail as possible (Figure 5.10). In order to capture maximum information, friction ridge detail from each finger and thumb will need to be recorded completely from one side of the fingernail to the other side of the fingernail. Furthermore, to minimize confusion and

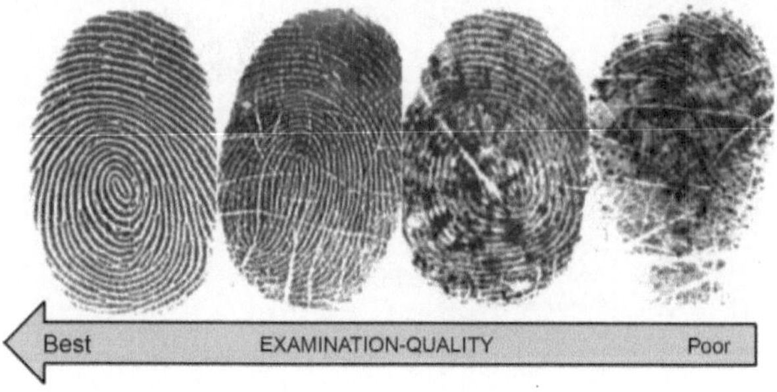

Figure 5.8 Reference of examination-quality to poor quality fingerprint impressions (SWGFAST et al., *2010).*

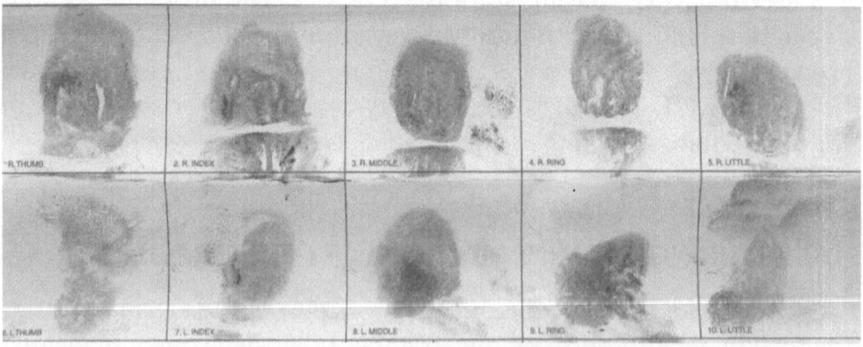

Figure 5.9a Poor-quality unacceptable fingerprint card (©NYC OCME, 2013).

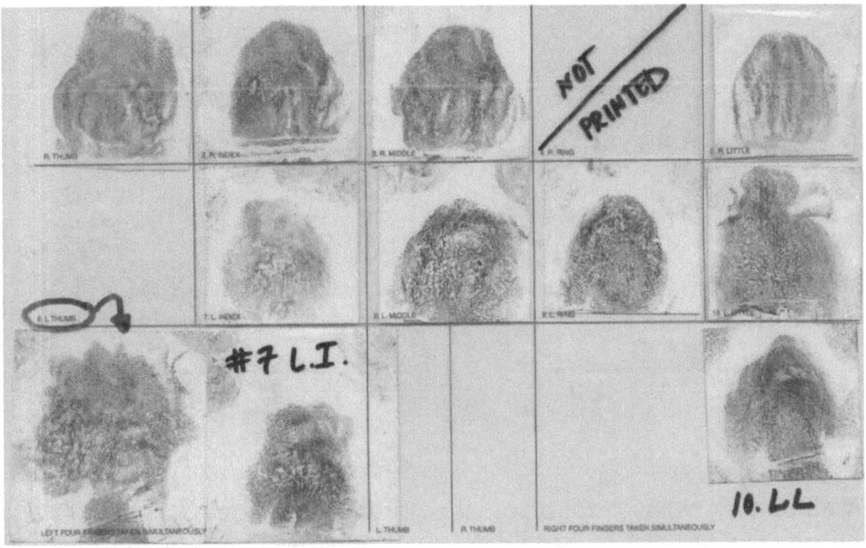

Figure 5.9b Reprinted high examination-quality fingerprint card (©NYC OCME, 2013).

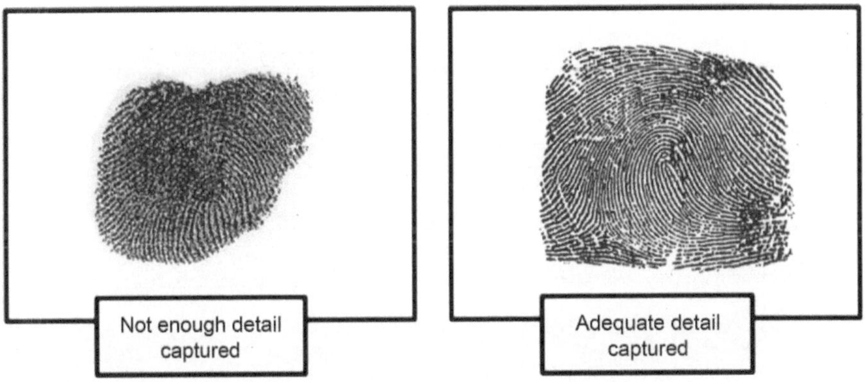

Figure 5.10 Not enough ridge detail captured and correct amount of ridge detail captured (©FBI, 2013).

ensure accuracy, fingerprint impressions from fingers and thumbs should be acquired using the acquisition medium or scanning device in the same sequence in which the spaces appear on the card, starting with the right thumb and ending with the left little finger.

When manually recording fingerprint impressions or using an electronic capture device, an important rule of thumb to remember is "less is more." Over-application of powder, ink, and/or pressure can lead to smudged fingerprint impressions that are indiscernible (Figure 5.11).

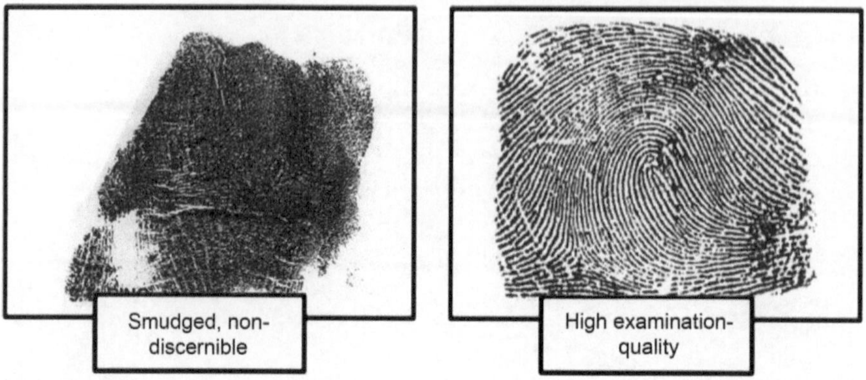

Figure 5.11 Smudged and non-discernible fingerprint impression and examination-quality fingerprint impression (©FBI, 2013).

Additionally, when using manual recording techniques, moisture present on the fingers may lead to smudged fingerprint impressions as well. On the other hand, slight moisture may aid in electronic fingerprint acquisition. Frequency of acquiring examination-quality impressions will increase with practice and experience.

CHAPTER 6

Overview of Antemortem (AM) Fingerprint Records in the United States

Contrary to the notion of a consolidated national fingerprint database that most current television shows promote, a single comprehensive and searchable database containing all fingerprint files does not exist in the United States. Current fingerprint databases used by the Medical Examiner/Coroner Offices and law enforcement agency communities tasked with forensic identification exist at the local, state, and federal levels and do not always overlap with regard to the information they contain. In addition, not all Medical Examiner/Coroner offices and law enforcement agencies possess the ability to access or search every one of these databases; a fact often unfamiliar to many forensic professionals who lack expertise in fingerprint searching and analysis techniques. If the forensic communities could better understand the strengths and limitations of available antemortem fingerprint databases and take measures to adequately search unidentified postmortem fingerprint records against these databases for humanitarian purposes, identification of postmortem fingerprint records would increase on a nationwide scale (Mulawka & Craig, 2011).

6.1 FEDERAL ANTEMORTEM FINGERPRINT DATABASES

Many agencies tasked with the forensic identification of unidentified human remains are unaware of three federal agencies that house the largest three fingerprint databases in the United States (Figure 6.1): the Federal Bureau of Investigation Criminal Justice Information Services Division (FBI CJIS), the Department of Homeland Security (DHS), and the Department of Defense Biometrics Identity Management Agency (DoD BIMA). The FBI CJIS houses a federal fingerprint database known as the Integrated Automated Fingerprint Identification System (IAFIS), which is currently being upgraded to the Next Generation Identification (NGI) Program. The DHS houses a federal fingerprint database known as the Automated Biometric Identification System (IDENT). The DoD BIMA houses a federal

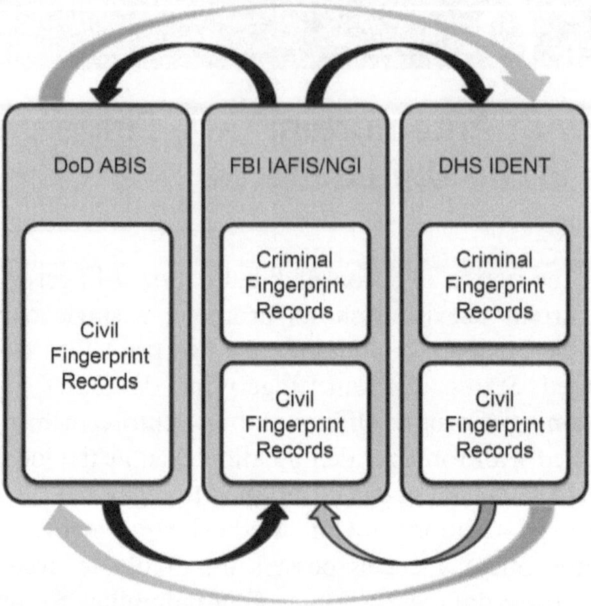

Figure 6.1 The triad of federal agencies that house the three largest fingerprint databases in the United States.

fingerprint database known as the Department of Defense Automated Biometric Identification System (DoD ABIS). Currently, the FBI is the only agency capable of searching both DHS IDENT and DoD ABIS databases. DHS can currently search FBI IAFIS/NGI only for special circumstances and cannot search DoD ABIS. DoD can currently search FBI IAFIS/NGI and cannot search DHS IDENT. Planned interoperability will allow DoD and DHS to share biometric data in the near future, which will complete the triad of FBI, DHS, and DoD biometrics information (Figure 6.2a,b). Through the Biometrics Triad, the FBI, DHS, and DoD, are working to achieve the interagency operability necessary for efficient sharing of biometrics data and contextual information (BIMA, 2010). All three federal agencies have fingerprint databases that are capable of performing broader searches and contain more antemortem fingerprint records than local or state agency fingerprint databases. As such, increased interoperability between these databases will increase the chances of identifying unidentified postmortem fingerprint records.

Most agencies are also unaware that the Federal Bureau of Investigation Criminal Justice Information Services Division Special

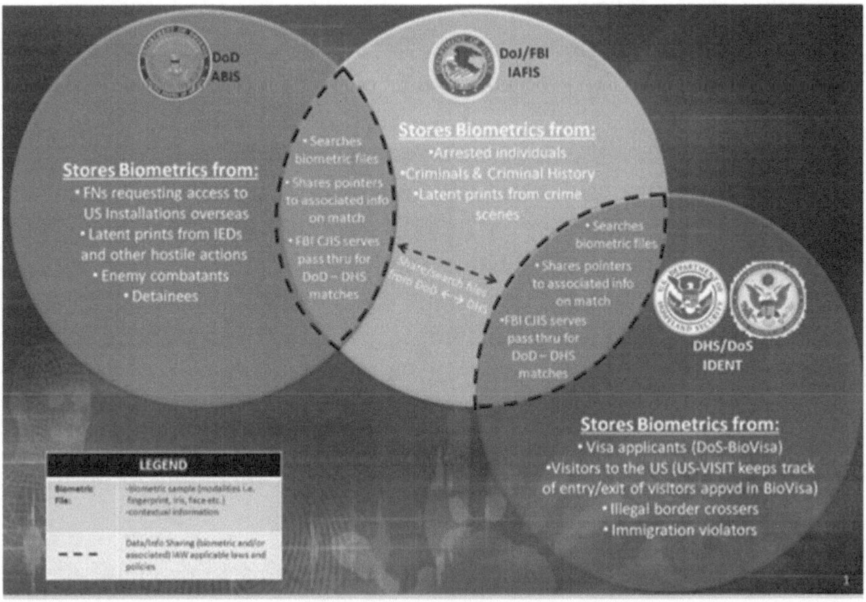

Figure 6.2a The current state of the Biometrics Triad (reprinted from DoD, 2010).

Figure 6.2b The desired-end state of the Biomentrics Triad (reprinted from DoD, 2010).

Processing Center (FBI CJIS SPC) and the Department of Homeland Security Biometric Support Center (DHS BSC) are available to assist local agencies with postmortem fingerprint identification efforts for humanitarian purposes. This can be very useful, especially if a local medical examiner or coroner's office is not affiliated with a law enforcement agency and thus does not have access to an automated fingerprint identification system (AFIS) terminal. Additionally, in 2009 the National Institute of Justice implemented the fully searchable National Missing and Unidentified Persons System (NamUs), which searches unidentified decedent information against missing person information in an effort to identify unidentified human remains and solve missing persons cases. NamUs assists Medical Examiner/Coroner Offices and law enforcement agencies across the United States with unidentified and missing person cases, as well as unidentified postmortem fingerprint identification efforts.

In 2008, a survey containing questions pertaining to unidentified and missing person protocols was distributed to Medical Examiner/Coroner offices and law enforcement agencies throughout the United States. Results of the survey revealed that 25% of Medical Examiner/Coroner Offices and law enforcement agencies do not submit unidentified postmortem fingerprint records to local agencies or to their state fingerprint bureau, 37% of Medical Examiner/Coroner offices and law enforcement agencies do not submit unidentified postmortem fingerprint records to the FBI CJIS SPC, and 69% of Medical Examiner/Coroner offices and law enforcement agencies do not submit unidentified postmortem fingerprint records to the DHS BSC (Mulawka).

In addition, most fingerprint databases were created for the purposes of criminal identification. As such, there are many restrictions in place when searching fingerprint databases due to privacy issues and laws on the local, state, and federal levels. When postmortem fingerprint records are searched, they are searched as criminal transactions and many times, only against criminal records. Furthermore, there are restrictions on retaining most civil fingerprint records and thus, many civil fingerprint records are either not accessible or not retainable. As such, fingerprint databases exist at local, state, federal, and private agency levels and the complex network (Figure 6.3) does not always overlap with the civil and criminal fingerprint records they contain.

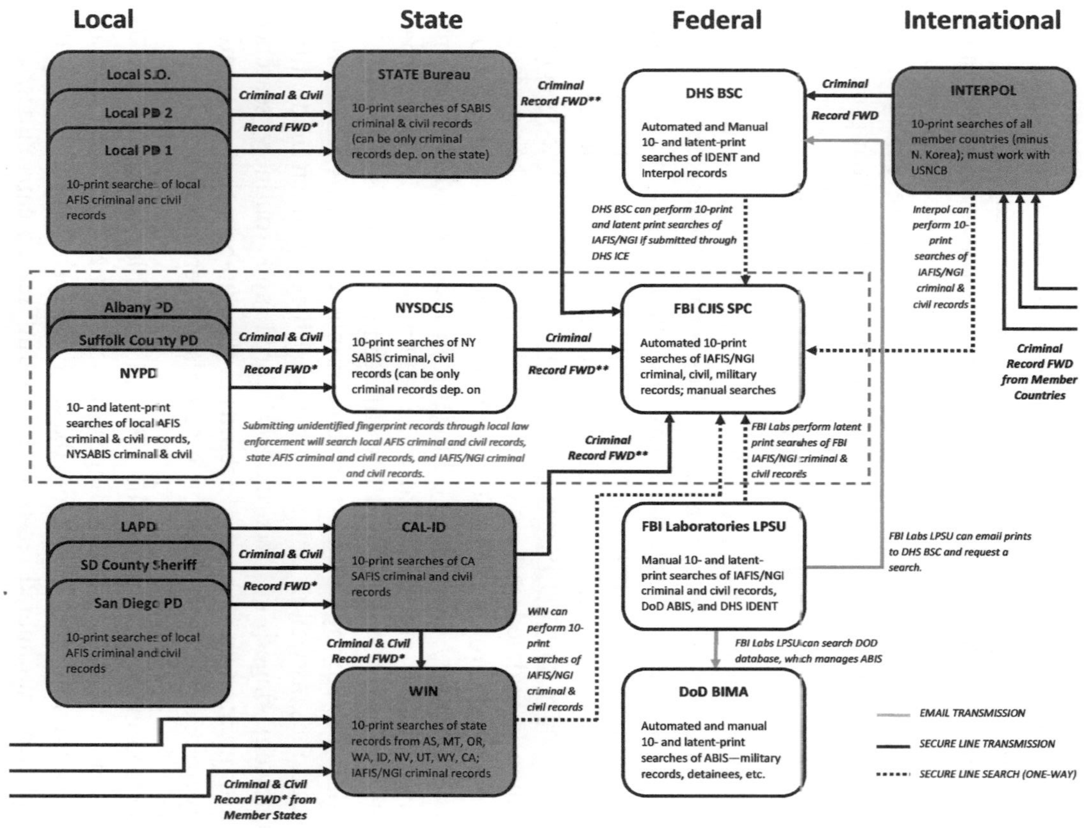

Figure 6.3 A snapshot of the complex network of fingerprint databases in the United States.

6.1.1 Federal Bureau of Investigation Criminal Justice Information Services Division Special Processing Center (FBI CJIS SPC), Integrated Automated Fingerprint Identification System (IAFIS), and Next Generation Identification (NGI) Program

The IAFIS is a national fingerprint and criminal history database, maintained by the FBI's CJIS Division, and responds to requests from local, state, and federal agencies 24 hours a day, 7 days a week, and year-round. The FBI has been the national fingerprint repository since 1924. The automated system was launched in 1999 to aid law enforcement agencies across the country in solving and preventing crime. Prior to the implementation of the automated database, ten-print processing was a lengthy and labor-intensive process, as each submission was classified and searched manually.

IAFIS is currently the largest biometric database in the world and holds over seventy-five million criminal records and corresponding fingerprints, as well as over thirty-six million civil, or non-criminal, fingerprint records. Civil fingerprints include individuals who are employed by the federal government and individuals who currently serve and have previously served in the U.S. military. The system is continuously updated with new fingerprint files that are being created and forwarded throughout various local, state, and federal jurisdictions across the country (Figure 6.4). Fingerprint records and criminal history information are submitted on a voluntary basis by more than 18,000 local, state, and federal law enforcement agencies (Figure 6.5). In addition to storing antemortem fingerprints records, IAFIS contains deceased files, as well as unknown deceased files, in which unidentified postmortem fingerprint records are stored and routinely searched against antemortem fingerprint records in the database that are continuously uploaded as new fingerprint records are generated.

Located in West Virginia, the FBI CJIS complex houses the IAFIS servers, as well as the physical fingerprint cards that have been scanned and entered into the IAFIS database. Fingerprint examiners in the SPC provide automated ten-print fingerprint search capabilities, electronic exchanges of fingerprints and responses, and electronic image storage with a rapid turnaround time on analyses. Examiners are able to rapidly search both criminal and civil fingerprint files that have been scanned into IAFIS. In addition, fingerprint examiners are able to perform manual searches through the physical fingerprint card

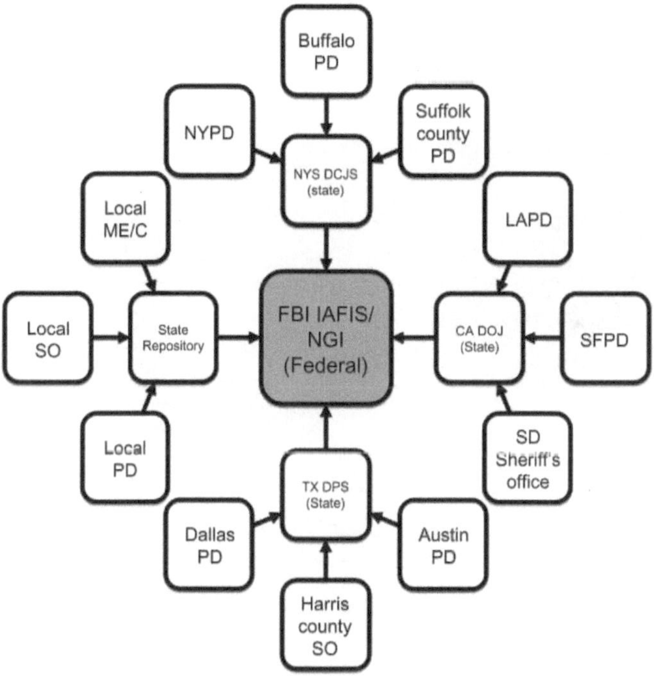

Figure 6.4 Snapshot of agencies submitting to FBI IAFIS/NGI.

records by classifying the unidentified fingerprint record and searching through physical antemortem fingerprint cards exhibiting a similar classification. Furthermore, any corresponding information to the fingerprint record can also be provided such as criminal histories, aliases, mug shots, photographs of scars and tattoos, and physical characteristics (height, weight, eye color, hair, etc.).

The FBI has recently initiated the Next Generation Identification (NGI) Program, which will further advance the FBI's biometric identification services. NGI will be deployed in multiple increments and eventually completely replace the current technical capabilities of IAFIS. It will introduce new functionality and state-of-the-art biometric identification services across a multi-year timeframe. The NGI Program is a collaborative effort between the FBI, CJIS Advisory Policy Board, as well as local, state, federal, and international members. Goals of the program include increased flexibility, capacity, accuracy, response times, availability, interoperability, and additional functionalities. More advanced fingerprint identification technologies will provide speedier and more efficient identification processing,

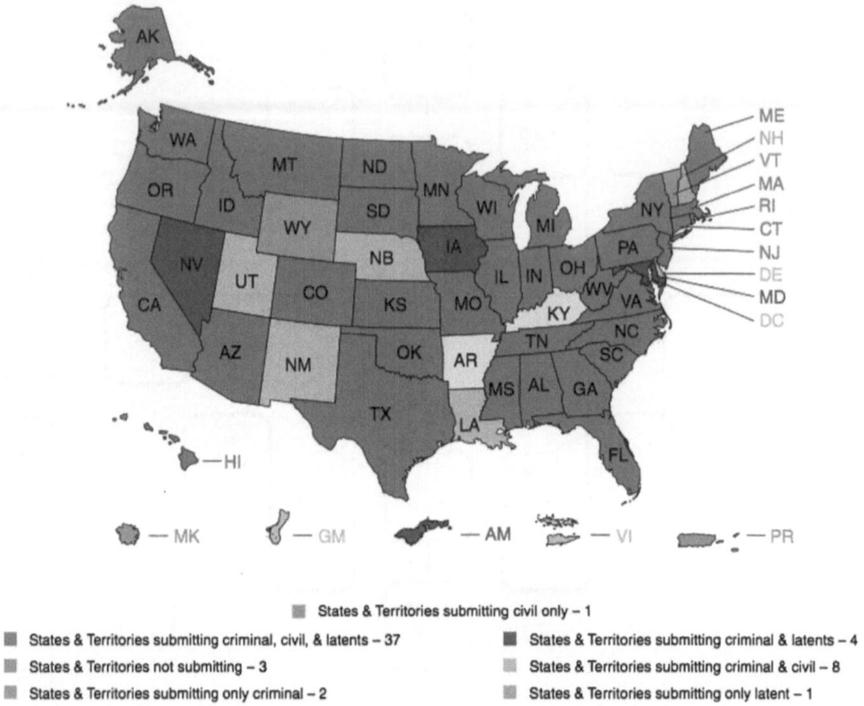

Figure 6.5 Electronic fingerprint submissions to IAFIS/NGI from each state. (reprinted from Fingerprint Sourcebook, 2012).

increased search accuracy, and improved latent processing services. More importantly, searches of ten-print submissions for non-criminal justice purposes will be processed much more smoothly. Advanced matching algorithms will improve ten-print search accuracy from 92% to 99.6%, as well as improved flat fingerprint searching. Advanced latent algorithms will provide more accurate latent print searches, which will be three times more accurate than they were using IAFIS. Additionally, the NGI Program will enhance integration of biometric data, thus creating a framework for a multimodal functionality that will serve to facilitate biometric identification. This multimodal system will promote information sharing, interoperability, and allow multimodal biometrics to be used for positive identification.

When fingerprints are submitted to the FBI and are not identified, they are not automatically forwarded to the latent print unit, which is in a different location from the ten-print unit. Latent fingerprint searches of IAFIS/NGI are conducted in a geographically separate location—the FBI Laboratory Latent Print Operations Unit (LPOU) in Quantico, Virginia. The LPOU conducts scientific examinations in friction ridge analysis, including the development and comparison of latent fingerprints, footprints, and palm prints. This unit has the ability to search IAFIS/NGI using a single latent print (ie. photograph of finger, photograph of casting, etc.) or a single inked/powdered print. A latent-print search request with the LPOU requires a separate process from a ten-print search request with SPC (FBI, 2013).

6.1.2 Department of Homeland Security Biometric Support Center (DHS BSC) Automated Biometric Identification System (IDENT)

The Department of Homeland Security Office of Biometric Identity Management (OBIM) was created in March 2013, replacing the United States Visitor and Immigration Status Indicator Technology (US-VISIT). The US-VISIT program was created in 2004 to support immigration and border management, providing visa-issuing posts and ports of entry with biometric technology that enabled the United States government to establish and verify identities of foreign visitors. US-VISIT's Biometric Support Center (BSC) helps many local, state, and federal agencies with ongoing investigations. BSC has access to over 100 million electronic fingerprint records in its Automated Biometric Identification System (IDENT). BSC has two fingerprint centers—BSC West and BSC East, one on each coast of the United States—that employ highly trained forensic analysts working 24 hours a day, 7 days a week, and year-round to verify biometrics, identify unidentified decedents, support terrorist investigations, and help solve crimes (DHS, 2013). When fingerprints are submitted to BSC and are not identified, they are then automatically forwarded on to the latent print unit, which is in the same location as the ten-print unit. This unit has the ability to search IDENT using a single latent print (ie. photograph of finger, photograph of casting, etc.) or a single inked/powdered print.

IDENT was developed by the Immigration and Naturalization Service (INS) in 1994 for the purpose of collecting and processing biometric information for law enforcement purposes. IDENT is now the central DHS-wide biometric and biographic repository that contains biometric records from visa applicants, border crossing card applicants, immigration benefit applicants, immigration violators, visitors to the United States, DHS credentialing applications, and criminal aliens. These records are created in United States points of entry, embassies, consulates, and border patrol stations. The biometric data includes digital fingerprints, iris scans, facial images, and photographs. It also links biometrics and biographic information for the purpose of establishing and verifying identities.

IDENT contains over seventy-five million records and approximately 70% of the records in the IDENT database are not replicated in any other local, state, or federal fingerprint database. IDENT includes fingerprints from high-profile subjects, wanted subjects, individuals apprehended by DHS, criminals, foreign nationals, terrorist watch lists, individuals applying for visas at U.S. Embassies around the world, travelers entering the U.S. with a visa or under the Visa Waiver program, and immigration violators. Biometric information is captured and verified at locations where visitors arrive and depart from U.S. air, sea, and land border ports, as well as visa-issuing posts across the world. Biometric and biographical information, as well as travel documents, are all authenticated using this program (Mulawka, 2008).

DHS and the FBI are in the process of establishing interoperability between IDENT and IAFIS/NGI through pilot programs with local and state law enforcement agencies. This will allow the complete, accurate, and timely exchange of biographic and biometric information between different agencies, thus ensuring that local, state, and federal law enforcement agencies, as well as immigration and authorized non-criminal justice agencies, can access correct information much more rapidly (DHS, 2013).

6.1.3 Department of Defense Biometrics Identity Management Agency (DoD BIMA) and Automated Biometric Identification System (ABIS)

The DoD ABIS is a national fingerprint and biometric repository maintained and operated by the DoD's Biometrics Identity Management Agency. The biometric repository contains data from multiple modalities, including fingerprint, palm print, iris, and facial recognition. BIMA employs Biometric Examiners (BEs) and Certified Latent Print Examiners (CLPEs) that respond to requests from local, state, and federal agencies 24 hours a day, 7 days a week, and year-round. ABIS holds over six million total records and corresponding fingerprints, and the Unsolved Latent Print File contains more than 200,000 files of latent prints from crime scenes or weapons caches

(BIMA, 2011). Currently, the DoD BIMA does not work with civilian agencies; however, it can be searched through the FBI.

6.1.4 National Missing and Unidentified Persons System (NamUs)

Shortly after the 9/11 attacks on the World Trade Center towers in New York City, the Department of Justice initiated a major effort to address an ongoing national issue in matching unidentified human remains with missing persons in the United States. In 2005, the National Institute of Justice (NIJ) gathered medical examiners, coroners, law enforcement agencies, forensic scientists, victim advocates, families of the missing, and policymakers to convene on this issue. The National Missing Persons Task Force was created as a result of the summit, which recommended improved quality, quantity, and access of information through a national repository. In 2007, the National Institute of Justice announced the development of the National Missing and Unidentified Persons System (NamUs), a searchable database developed to assist Medical Examiner/Coroner Offices across the United States identify unidentified human remains and link them to missing person cases. The NamUs reporting and searching system improved the consistency, quality, and quantity of data regarding these cases. Medical Examiner/Coroner Offices, law enforcement agencies, forensic professionals, families of missing persons, and the general public were provided with access to NamUs. The database serves as a repository for contextual and scientific information such as weight, height, scars, tattoos, clothing, fingerprints, dental charting, and DNA information.

There are two sections of NamUs that search one another with the information they contain—the Missing Persons Database and the Unidentified Persons database. The Missing Persons Database can be populated by anyone, but the information is verified before it is posted. This database provides many resources, including free biometric collection and testing assistance, as well as the ability to print missing person information. Additionally, there are links to Medical Examiner/Coroner Offices, state clearinghouses, law enforcement agencies, related legislation, and victim assistance groups. The Unidentified Persons Database is populated only by Medical Examiner/Coroner Offices, but can be searched by anyone using certain criteria, such as race, sex, etc. (NamUS, 2013). The Unidentified Persons database also provides a section for entering fingerprint classification for all ten fingers, as well as a section for uploading an electronic image of the postmortem records. Once uploaded, NamUs staff facilitates fingerprint database searches and fingerprint comparisons. NamUs training and continuing education underlines that "it is not sufficient to have your unidentified remains prints run only through your local or state fingerprint databases and that postmortem fingerprints should always be run through two federal fingerprint agencies—FBI SPC and DHS BSC" (NamUs, 2012).

6.2 WESTERN IDENTIFICATION NETWORK (WIN)

The Western Identification Network, Inc. (WIN) is a multi-state, nonprofit, AFIS network created in 1988 by a consortium of ten Western state and local law enforcement agencies. This high-speed multi-state Automated Fingerprint Identification System was created with the purpose of providing services to multiple jurisdictions that no single state or local agency could cost-effectively provide. WIN has the ability to digitize, store, and compare criminal and civil fingerprint information from submitting agencies. Fingerprint records are provided by the states of Alaska, California, Idaho, Montana, Nevada, Oregon, Utah, Washington, and Wyoming. Other contributing agencies include the FBI, DHS, Internal Revenue Service (IRS), Drug Enforcement Administration (DEA), Postal Inspection Service, and the Secret Service. Members of WIN have access to over twenty-nine million fingerprint records of the Western United States (Western Identification Network, 2012).

6.3 STATE AND LOCAL FINGERPRINT DATABASES

Although the FBI manages the national repository of fingerprint records, only a percent of the population's records are contained in the system. Additionally, only a portion of information related to these records and those not indexed with the FBI are available at state and local levels only. Each local law enforcement agency submits criminal fingerprint records through its respective state. The state will then forward certain criminal records to the FBI IAFIS/NGI (Figure 6.6). Additionally, civil fingerprint records are forwarded to the state through local law enforcement or government agencies, but will reside at the state bureau and are not forwarded to the FBI. Furthermore, civil records may be designated as retainable or non-retainable.

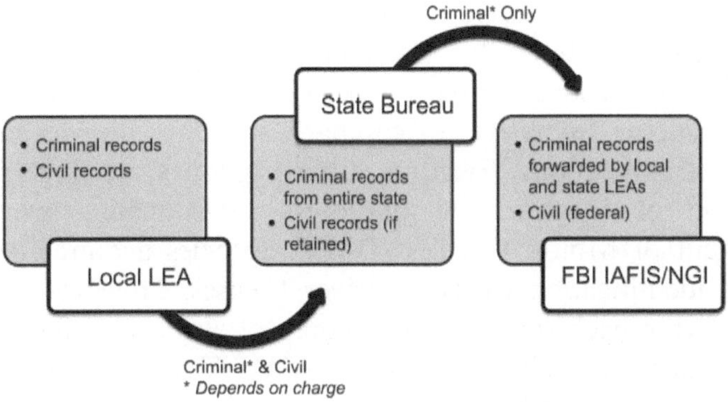

Figure 6.6 Local agencies submit to FBI IAFIS/NGI through their respective State Bureau.

Certain civil records are retained at the state level. On the contrary, some civil records may only be cascaded against criminal records and then expunged; these are known as non-retainable.

State record repositories have also made their records available for non-criminal justice agencies. Some states allow more access than others based on the notion that their records are public records and should therefore be accessible by the public. On the other hand, other states are more restrictive with many of their records, limiting their use for non-criminal justice purposes to those specifically authorized by state legislation. Additionally, many state-maintained records may be more complete, accurate, and up-to-date than the records maintained at the FBI level. As such, searching both state and federal databases will yield more comprehensive data.

The only way to gain access to many of these records is to search other state and local databases separately. Currently, the capabilities to search unidentified postmortem fingerprint records against another state or neighboring local database is very limited. The lack of interoperability between these databases reduces the opportunities for fingerprint identifications throughout the United States. It is estimated that one in five criminals has a criminal record in more than one state (WIN, 2012). These statistics form the basis for supporting a national policy of conducting both state and national fingerprint searches in order to obtain as complete and accurate a search as possible. The deficiencies in fingerprint database interoperability have even been recognized by the National Academies report, Strengthening Forensic Science in the United States: A Path Forward (2009).

Various other states, local administrative regions, agencies, and private businesses have their own fingerprint databases used for an assortment of reasons—applicant background checks, receipt of credentials, benefits, homeless services, bank accounts, fitness centers, and many more institutions. Even recent smartphones use fingerprints for verification of identification purposes. Additionally, some states' Department of Motor Vehicles (DMV) agencies acquire fingerprints for state identification cards or driver licenses. However, the DMV varies between each state, and therefore not every state database contains similarly accessible data. The DMV office in the desired state must be contacted and asked if any fingerprints are obtained during application for a driver license or state identification card. However, many of these databases are not searchable databases and are not linked to an AFIS or any other searchable fingerprint database. That is, they are only searchable by text fields, not by the fingerprint information. Therefore, an unknown postmortem fingerprint cannot be searched against these types of databases. Only if a tentative name is known can the associated antemortem fingerprint record be located if it exists in the database. Consequently, a tentative name must be available to perform a search and possible comparison to be performed. An even further setback is that most law enforcement agencies do not possess the ability to search many of these databases due to privacy issues. Lastly, most private institutions are more reluctant to release fingerprint records due to the potential for litigation.

6.4 FOREIGN FINGERPRINT DATABASES

Many other international agencies, such as the International Criminal Police Organization (INTERPOL), populate and maintain their own fingerprint databases. Automated Fingerprint Identification Systems are used in many foreign countries such as United Kingdom, Canada, Australia, Italy, Israel, Venezuela, Algeria, Argentina, Chile, Pakistan, and Turkey. Additionally, the European Union (EU) created EURODAC in 2003, a fingerprint identification system used in all EU member states, Norway, and Iceland. EURODAC contains fingerprints of illegal immigrants and asylum seekers. Unfortunately, law enforcement agencies in the United States do not possess the ability to electronically search databases in foreign jurisdictions; however, a formal request can be made through INTERPOL via the United States National Central Bureau in Washington DC.

CHAPTER 7

Submission of PM Fingerprint Records for Automated Fingerprint Identification System (AFIS) Searches and Antemortem Fingerprint Record Investigation

Out of all scientific modalities used in forensic human identification, fingerprint identification is the most rapid and cost-effective means by which to identify unidentified human remains (UHR). However, there is a common misconception that if an individual was fingerprinted at some point in life, an antemortem fingerprint record resides in a national, comprehensive, and searchable database of all criminal and civil fingerprint records. Unfortunately, this is not the case—antemortem fingerprint records must be located within a complex network of searchable and non-searchable databases, or must be specially requested for specific reasons because the records reside in a private institution. When a forensic examiner or law enforcement official is tasked with the forensic identification of unidentified postmortem fingerprint records, the complexity of antemortem fingerprint investigation, searching, and comparison must be understood. The examiner or investigator must gather certain information in order to know where to search for the possible antemortem fingerprint record. Measures must be taken to use all available resources, leverage all fingerprint databases, and increase federal submission capabilities in order to exhaust all avenues in the attempt to identify postmortem fingerprint records.

7.1 AUTOMATED FINGERPRINT IDENTIFICATION SYSTEM (AFIS) SEARCHES OF POSTMORTEM FINGERPRINT RECORDS

Simply because an individual was fingerprinted does not mean that person's fingerprint record exists or resides in a searchable database. The term "searchable database" may also be misleading. A database may be searchable only by the text field (i.e. name). Therefore, the antemortem fingerprint record can only be accessed if a tentative name is known. It is important to know if a fingerprint database is an Automated Fingerprint Identification System (AFIS), which is searchable by the fingerprint data. During an AFIS search of an unidentified postmortem fingerprint record, the postmortem fingerprint data is searched against antemortem fingerprint data (*Explained in more detail in Section 7.1.2*).

The largest searchable automated fingerprint identification databases were created for the purposes of criminal identification. As such, when unidentified postmortem fingerprint records are searched, they are processed and searched as criminal transactions. Instead, the records should be searched against all available fingerprint records for humanitarian purposes; just because a person dies due to unnatural circumstances and falls under the jurisdiction of the medical examiner, it does not imply the individual was a criminal. Ironically, because postmortem fingerprint records are mostly searched against criminal record databases, it is currently beneficial to be a criminal for a higher probability of postmortem fingerprint identification.

There are also many restrictions in place when searching fingerprint databases due to privacy issues and laws on the local, state, and federal levels. Many law enforcement agencies (LEAs) are hesitant to allow access to their local fingerprint databases due to sensitivity of criminal record information attached to fingerprint records. Unidentified postmortem fingerprint records must be forwarded electronically to LEAs for searching and identification purposes only. Access to the criminal record is not necessary, but can be beneficial in locating and notifying next-of-kin for proper release and burial or cremation of remains.

Additionally, there are strict restrictions on retaining most civil fingerprint records and thus, many civil fingerprint records are either not accessible or not retainable. If the civil fingerprint records are retainable, they usually reside at the state level and the majority of them cannot be accessed electronically by other states. For example, if a postmortem fingerprint from a local jurisdiction in Illinois is electronically searched via local submission, it is cascaded against a local fingerprint database, then the Illinois State fingerprint database, and finally the FBI IAFIS/NGI; it will not be searched against civil records retained in another state. Furthermore, there is a lack of knowledge by many agencies tasked with forensic identification of unidentified human remains about the fact that submission of unidentified postmortem fingerprint records to local law enforcement agencies currently fails to search antemortem fingerprint records from the Department of Homeland Security (DHS). Approximately 70% of the fingerprint records in the DHS database are

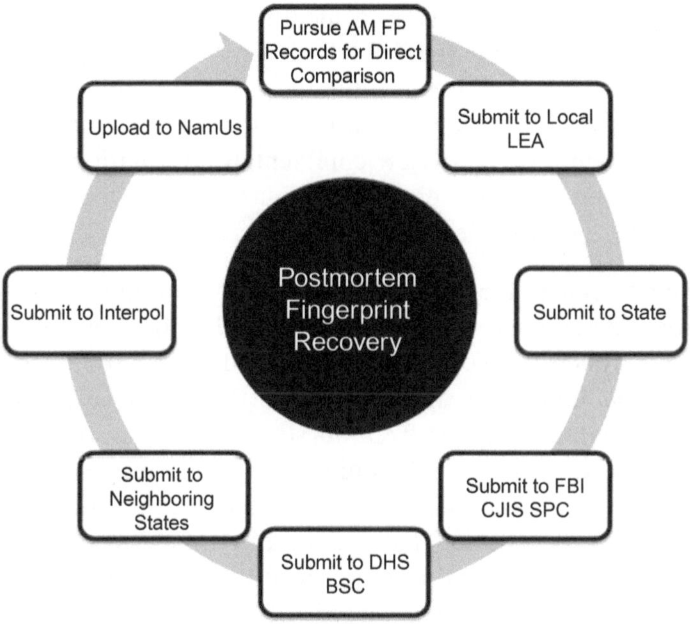

Figure 7.1 Postmortem fingerprint submission strategy (Mulawka & DePaolo, 2013).

not replicated in any other federal, state, or local fingerprint databases. Consequently, many antemortem fingerprint records are missed when searching unidentified deceased records electronically. Using the current electronic procedure fails to perform a thorough search of all available fingerprint databases in an attempt to identify the unidentified decedent. Due to this gap in interoperability, if the Medical Examiner/Coroner Office (ME/C) is located in a jurisdiction that is frequented by residents of other states, a separate manual submission should be performed to search the surrounding state fingerprint repositories. As a result, an unidentified Postmortem Fingerprint Submission Strategy (Figure 7.1) should be developed and followed to submit to the appropriate local, state, federal, and international agencies in order to perform an adequate and thorough search of all available fingerprint records.

7.1.1 Obtaining an Unrestricted Originating Agency Identification Number

In order for an agency to request electronic fingerprint searches, the agency must have an Originating Agency Identification (ORI) Number, a nine-character identifier assigned to a specific agency. The ORI number is a code assigned by the FBI or a state's main law enforcement agency and serves to identify the agency that has originated a request. The unique ORI is usually a 9-digit alpha-numeric code consisting of 2 digits identifying the state, followed by 6–7 numerals, and could possibly end with a letter. Once an agency obtains an ORI, it is authorized to view confidential information due to state and federal statutes; however, it is not authorized to share the results with any other person or entity.

Law enforcement agencies have the ability to obtain an unrestricted ORI allowing them access to the Interstate Identification Index (III or "Triple I") system, which is an automated criminal history record repository maintained by the FBI. The III System is a segment of IAFIS and contains records from all states and territories, as well as from federal and international criminal justice agencies. All of the state records in the III System are submitted to the FBI through the central criminal record repositories that receive all criminal records submitted by all or most of the local criminal justice agencies in their jurisdictions. The III System contains records of persons arrested for felonies or misdemeanors under either state or federal law. The index includes identification data such as name, race, gender, and birth date. The system also contains FBI and state identification numbers (SIDs) from every state that has a record for that individual. The records in the III System are all based on ten-print antemortem fingerprint records, which are used for searching. When a request is made, data is automatically retrieved from the appropriate repositories, including state repositories, and then forwarded to the requesting agency's ORI (US DOJ OAG, 2006).

The FBI IAFIS was initially created for the use of government agencies involved in the administration of criminal justice functions. As the system evolved over time, the FBI authorized some access for certain non-criminal justice purposes. The use of FBI criminal history records by non-criminal justice agencies is usually done by a government agency that applies suitability criteria that have been established by legislation. If there is no legislation available, a non-criminal justice agency without an unrestricted ORI, such as a Medical Examiner/Coroner Office, should work with its affiliated law enforcement agency. If the ME/C Office is not affiliated with a law enforcement agency, a different type of ORI may be requested that allows the agency to perform fingerprint searches for humanitarian purposes. However, the ME/C Office will not be able to gain access to the III

System, unless there is legislation available stating otherwise. Once the ME/C Office obtains the ORI, manual fingerprint searches of the state and FBI IAFIS/NGI will be possible. In addition, electronic fingerprint searches of the local, state and FBI IAFIS/NGI will be possible by establishing a secure line connection, as well as an Automated Fingerprint Identification System (AFIS) terminal.

7.1.2 Automated Fingerprint Identification Technology, the ANSI-NIST Standard, and Electronic Submissions

With the rapid advancement of technology, local, state, and federal criminal justice agencies have acquired equipment and implemented systems to facilitate fingerprint acquisition, searching, and identification through digital means. The majority of fingerprint records are now acquired using flatbed scanners, automated fingerprint identification systems (AFIS), and livescan fingerprint devices. AFIS terminals use flatbed scanners to scan physical fingerprint cards into digital images and store them as electronic files. Livescan fingerprint devices scan the friction ridge detail directly from the fingers and process the images to extract specific features. The digital record created can then be compared against databases containing previously acquired images. The results from these comparisons yield potential candidate identifications that must be viewed by human fingerprint examiners to make the final determination of identification. As there are many different biometric databases (explained in detail in Chapter 6), a standard was needed to designate a common format that would allow the effective exchange of identification data in multiple jurisdictions or systems created by different manufacturers (NIST, 2000).

Beginning in 1991, the National Institute of Standards and Technology (NIST) hosted a series of workshops with forensic experts, fingerprint repository managers, consultants, and industry representatives to develop a national standard for the exchange of fingerprint data that also complied with the American National Standards Institute (ANSI) guidelines. In 1993, the ANSI/NIST standard was approved and officially named the "Data Format for the Interchange of Fingerprint Information (ANSI NIST-CSL 1-1993)." The standard and its subsequent revisions, currently the ANSI/NIST-Information Technology Laboratory 1-2011 (ANSI/NIST-ITL 1-2011) standard, became commonly known in the fingerprint world as the "ANSI/NIST standard." After the ANSI-NIST standard was approved, the FBI published the Electronic Fingerprint Transmission

Specification (EFTS) in 1994, which specified which Transaction Types (TOTs), data fields, and record types the FBI would accept. The EFTS also specified which data fields in the ANSI-NIST standard where mandatory, and which were optional. Interpol developed an Interpol implementation of the ANSI-NIST standard and other countries soon followed to adopt the Interpol Implementation (Komarinski, 2005).

If everything was implemented correctly and in full compliance with the ANSI-NIST standard, as well as EFTS specifications, digital fingerprints collected by any compliant vendor's device could be read by any other compliant AFIS and most importantly, the FBI's IAFIS. The FBI later appended the EFTS with an image quality standard (IQS) known as Appendix F. The IQS defined the minimal acceptable standards for any equipment used to capture digital fingerprints. As other countries adopted the ANSI/NIST standard, EFTS was used as a model and the IQS standard was also incorporated. The EFTS was eventually expanded upon and became the Electronic Biometric Transmission Specification (EBTS) and included additional biometric modalities to recognize the rapidly developing biometric identification industry (Pato & Millett, 2010).

The Medical Examiner/Coroner (ME/C) system varies from state to state throughout the United States (Hickman *et al.*, 2007), and as a result, some ME/C offices are not affiliated with their local or state law enforcement agencies (LEA). If this is the case, the ME/C office may be designated as a non-criminal justice agency. Often, this may mean the ME/C office does not have an Automated Fingerprint Identification System (AFIS) terminal and thus, no direct electronic access to a local AFIS database, which would in turn allow access to the state and federal fingerprint databases detailed in Chapter 6. In these instances, postmortem fingerprint records must be physically transported to a local LEA for searching, which can often be a cumbersome and labor-intensive process. Alternatively, the record can be scanned with a regular offline flatbed scanner and emailed to the LEA, but will then have to be printed and scanned into an AFIS terminal, which can reduce the quality of the original postmortem fingerprint record. Often, the original fingerprint record is of a reduced quality due to the condition of the remains. In addition, when the LEA performs the search of the postmortem fingerprint record, the record may be treated as a criminal record and consequently may not be adequately searched against all available antemortem records. The record must be searched for humanitarian purposes as an unknown deceased fingerprint record.

If a non-LEA affiliated ME/C has the funding to purchase an AFIS terminal, the agency will have the ability to capture postmortem fingerprints using a livescan device. In addition, an online cardscan device will allow the scanning and conversion of any manually acquired fingerprint records (i.e. in a situation where the condition of the remains requires manual fingerprint processing using advanced techniques) into the ANSI/NIST standard and EBTS-compliant format. This will allow for the electronic fingerprint transmission and subsequent searches of the local, state, and FBI IAFIS/NGI repositories via a secure line connection. In order to establish the secure line connection to local and state databases, the ME/C must obtain permission from the corresponding local and state agencies; access to FBI IAFIS/NGI will be granted by the state. However, using only this process will still fail to adequately search the record against all available antemortem records. The record will still have to be searched against other databases that may not be accessible using the secure line connection, such as DHS or other state bureaus. In these cases, the fingerprint record may have to be submitted manually.

Each external agency may have different submission procedures and must be contacted individually. The AFIS terminal will scan the fingerprint record into a format that can only be viewed using specialized software that will be accessible on the AFIS terminal. However, the record can also be viewed using NIST-viewing software or the FBI's Universal Latent Workstation (ULW) software. Other agencies may require a more compatible format, just as JPEG, JPEG2000, TIFF, or PDF files. The AFIS terminal software may be configured to convert the ANSI-NIST file into one or all of these formats. Once converted, the images may be viewed on most computer workstations and are compatible with many different programs. Once the electronic postmortem fingerprint record is created, it should be stored in an internal case management system or database (Chapter 8) and searched against all available fingerprint databases (Chapter 6).

7.1.3 Transaction Type and Wording of Manual Submissions

A plethora of antemortem fingerprint records are missed when searching unidentified postmortem records electronically; therefore, a separate manual submission should be performed to search the surrounding state fingerprint repositories in the event that an electronic submission yields negative results. This process will ensure that a thorough search is performed of all available fingerprint databases in an attempt to identify the unidentified decedent. In addition, if an agency is only capable of performing manual submissions, it is important to specify the Type of Transaction (TOT) and ensure the submission is worded correctly. The TOT and wording of the request can designate what fingerprint databases are searched.

Electronic ten-print submissions originate from AFIS terminals at either the local, state, or federal levels. Local submissions are processed by a local AFIS and electronically transmitted to a state identification bureau for processing. In the event an identification, or "ident," is made at the state level, an ident response will be transmitted back to the local agency and, depending on the TOT, may be forwarded to the FBI for processing. There are several types of electronic ten-print submissions that are accepted by the FBI:

TOT	Transaction
CAR	Criminal Ten-Print Submission (Answer Required)
CNA	Criminal Ten-Print Submission (No Answer Necessary)
FANC	Federal Applicant (No Charge)
FAUF	Federal Applicant User Fee
NFAP	Non-Federal Advanced Payment
NFUF	Non-Federal Applicant User Fee
MAP	Miscellaneous Applicant Civil
DEK	Known Deceased
DEU	Unknown Deceased
MPR	Missing Person
AMN	Amnesia Victim

Source: (©*FBI 2005*)

Known Deceased, or DEK transactions, are submitted for a decedent whose identity is known. If the postmortem fingerprint record is determined to be identical to an antemortem fingerprint record in the state repository or IAFIS/NGI, the antemortem record will be marked as deceased. DEU, or Unknown Deceased transactions, are submitted for a decedent whose identity is unknown. If the postmortem fingerprint record is determined to be identical to an antemortem fingerprint record in the state repository or IAFIS/NGI, the antemortem record will be marked as deceased and the results will be sent to the state bureau and contributor of the postmortem fingerprint record. In the event of negative results, the postmortem fingerprint record will be assigned an FBI number and added to the criminal file as an unknown postmortem fingerprint record in order to be periodically searched against antemortem fingerprint records that are continuously being uploaded into IAFIS/NGI. In addition, a search of the civil file will be conducted with a DEU transaction since it is being searched for humanitarian purposes.

Upon manual submission to any fingerprint database, it should be underlined that the postmortem record is being searched for humanitarian purposes and specified that the record should be searched against all available databases (criminal, civil, military, etc.). The postmortem record must not be searched as a criminal record only, as this will fail to perform a thorough search of all available fingerprint databases. In addition, the postmortem record should be marked as "yes" for retention in the event that results are negative. This will ensure the postmortem record is retained in IAFIS/NGI for periodic searching. Furthermore, any special circumstances for acquiring the fingerprint impressions should be noted, such as photographs of fingers or skin (which are positive impressions and must be reversed since an acquired or deposited fingerprint impression is a negative impression), photographs of castings, dermal impressions (which should be enlarged), degloved epidermal impressions (which should be reduced), etc. Lastly, it is crucial to request that a latent-print search is performed in the event that a ten-print search yields negative results.

Submission Request Summary
1. All unidentified postmortem fingerprint submissions must include "DEU Transaction" for the TOT
2. Ensure all available databases are searched (criminal, civil, military, etc.)
3. Ensure unidentified postmortem record is marked as retained
4. Include any special circumstances during fingerprint acquisition
5. In the event of negative results during ten-print search, must be forwarded for latent-print search

7.1.4 Retention of Fingerprint Records

Retention ensures that a fingerprint record is retained in an agency's database for the purpose of continual searching. Retention times differ between local, state, and federal agencies. Policies and legislation dictate most retention times. Certain agencies, such as the New York State Division of Criminal Justice Services, retain only identified postmortem fingerprint records indefinitely. In addition, unidentified postmortem fingerprint records are currently expunged after approximately one year. On the contrary, the FBI IAFIS/NGI retains unidentified postmortem fingerprint records indefinitely, while identified postmortem fingerprint records are eventually expunged from the system. Retention of a fingerprint record can be confirmed by obtaining the FBI number assigned to the unidentified postmortem fingerprint record, which should reside in the electronic fingerprint response. Unfortunately, ensuring that an unidentified postmortem record is marked for retention can only occur on an electronic submission that is transmitted through the state bureau. The state bureau is the conduit to the FBI IAFIS/NGI for all fingerprint records coming from local jurisdictions. Therefore, any unidentified postmortem fingerprint records should be resubmitted periodically to the agencies that do not retain unidentified postmortem fingerprint records (Chapter 9). If the unidentified postmortem fingerprint record is ever submitted to IAFIS/NGI for any reason, it should theoretically be a match to itself and the associated FBI number. In the event that an identification is effected on a previously unidentified postmortem fingerprint record that was retained in IAFIS/NGI, the FBI will notify the contributing agency of the identification. Should the unidentified decedent be identified via other means by the contributing agency, the agency should notify the FBI to remove the unidentified postmortem fingerprint record and provide confirming documentation, such as a death certificate.

7.1.5 Manual, Automated, Ten-Print, and Latent Fingerprint Searches

Fingerprint matching can be defined as the "exercise of finding the similarity or dissimilarity in any two given fingerprint images" (NIJ, 2012). Before the introduction of Automated Fingerprint Identification Systems (AFIS), fingerprint matching was a manual process performed by trained fingerprint examiners. Manual fingerprint classification was developed to sort fingerprints by physiological characteristics in order to search one fingerprint record against many fingerprint records to find a potential match. The Henry Classification System gained worldwide acceptance in 1899 and allowed for logical categorization of ten-print fingerprint records based on fingerprint pattern types. This system was developed to reduce the effort required to search large numbers of fingerprint records.

Manual searches using this system allowed examiners to search unknown fingerprints against known fingerprints and either include or exclude potential candidates.

As local, state, and federal agencies received and retained more and more fingerprint records, manual fingerprint classification became time-consuming and labor intensive. The need for a more efficient means of fingerprint classification and searching became crucial. As a result, automated fingerprint matching algorithms and systems were created, which proved to be a reliable, rapid, consistent, and cost-effective solution that significantly reduced the work of fingerprint examiners. The systems executed an automated process of matching unknown fingerprint records against a database of known and unknown fingerprint records. Current automated systems utilize algorithms that interpret the flow of the overall ridges to assign a fingerprint classification, extract the minutiae detail, and search for similarities between any two given sets of minutiae in a large repository. Automated searches are performed at tens of thousands of records per second. The results are sorted according to a score designated by the degree of similarity, as well as any other available characteristics and criteria that may further filter potential candidates. This can all occur without human expert intervention when the fingerprint record is of good quality, since the matching can be highly accurate. This is known as a "lights-out" identification, which refers to the system requiring minimal or zero human assistance to make the match. Depending on the quality of the fingerprint image and the application being used, a matching algorithm can expedite a large amount of fingerprint identifications, especially if the fingerprint records being searched are of very high examination-quality.

Nevertheless, the automatic fingerprint matching algorithms are not as accurate and cannot replicate the complex decision-making of a well-trained fingerprint examiner. If the fingerprint record is of very poor quality, a matching algorithm may not be as accurate as the fingerprint examiner. Nevertheless, the matching algorithm may yield possible matches, with a sample size that is much smaller than the size of the database being searched. The fingerprint examiner then only has to manually search a smaller number of fingerprints to try and find a match.

A ten-print fingerprint record is known as a record of all ten fingerprints, which includes one print taken from each finger that has been rolled from one edge of the nail to the other, plain (or slap) impressions of each of the four fingers of each hand, and plain impressions of each thumb. A ten-print record is acquired using livescan or traditional recording methods and usually is of higher examination-quality than a latent fingerprint record. A latent fingerprint record is known to be of low examination-quality, and may be smudged or blurred. A latent fingerprint may capture only a small area of the finger and can have large nonlinear distortions. As such, trained latent fingerprint examiners typically manually mark certain features in latent fingerprints. Latent fingerprint matching requires substantial human intervention through a procedure known as ACE-V—analysis, comparison, evaluation and verification. Manually matching a latent print against a large repository is not possible. Automated systems have made latent searches of large fingerprint repositories possible. Unique features are manually marked by examiners and entered into the AFIS system for automated searching. The latent fingerprint is searched using the examiner's designated criteria and a candidate list is generated and returned. The candidate fingerprints are then compared and verified by latent fingerprint examiners. A second latent fingerprint examiner verifies any identification

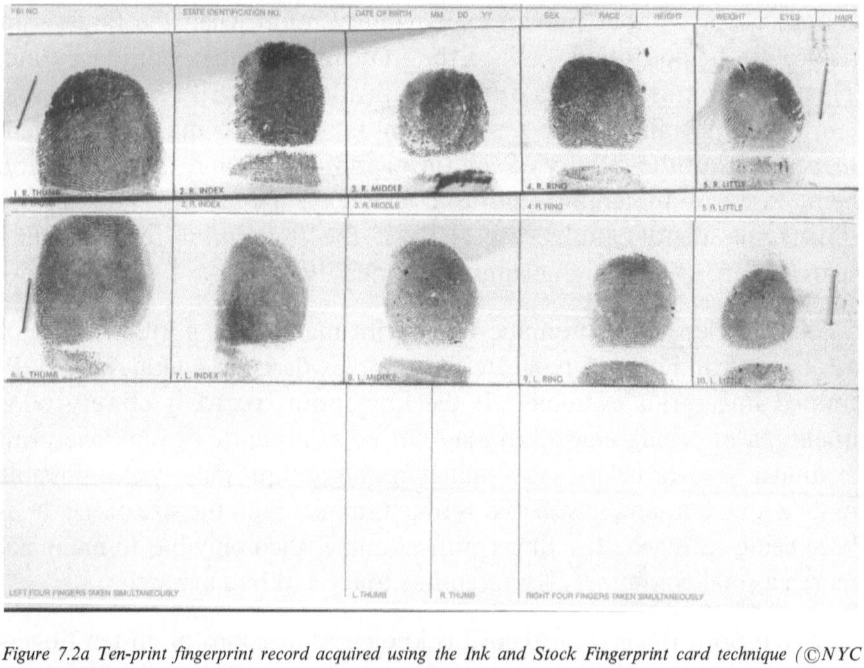

Figure 7.2a Ten-print fingerprint record acquired using the Ink and Stock Fingerprint card technique (©NYC OCME, 2012).

made. Unfortunately, the features marked by examiners are not always compatible with those that are automatically extracted by AFIS. This can result in reduced matching accuracy. Latent fingerprints can also be matched against a small number of known fingerprints if the other circumstantial information (tentative name, gender, age, etc.) reduces the pool of records to be compared against.

When applied to postmortem fingerprint records, creating a ten-print fingerprint record is the ideal form of acquisition, as this will result in efficient and rapid automated searching. A ten-print postmortem fingerprint record is created when the fingerprint impressions are recorded on a ten-print fingerprint card using any of the Postmortem Fingerprint Recovery Techniques described in Chapters 3 and 4. The ten-print fingerprint record can contain fingerprint impressions acquired using the Ink and Stock Fingerprint Card Technique (Figure 7.2a), Powder/Acetate Fingerprint Card/Adhesive Lifter Technique (Figure 7.2b), Livescan

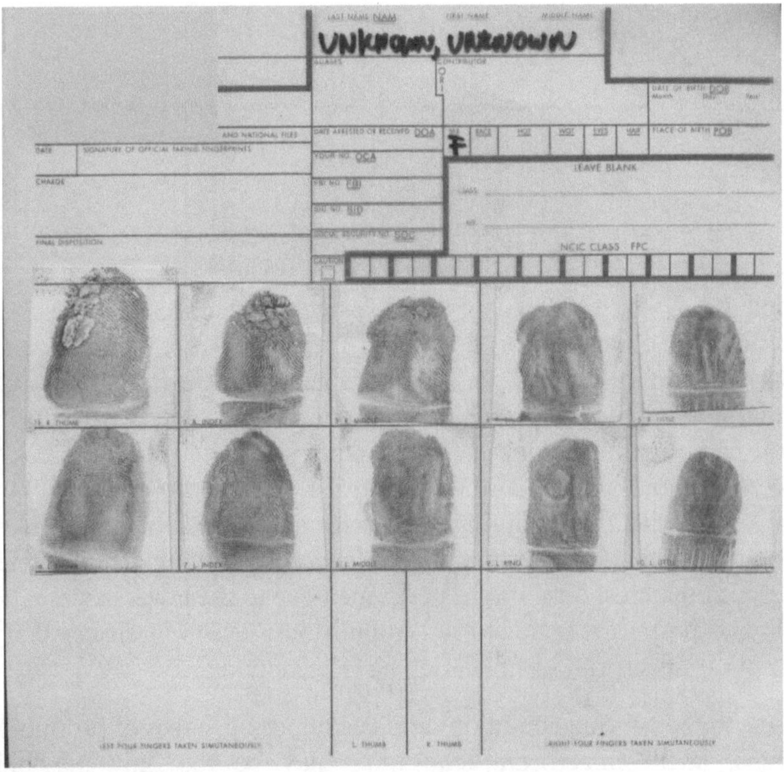

Figure 7.2b Ten-print fingerprint record acquired using the Powder/Acetate Fingerprint Card/Adhesive Lifter Technique (©NYC OCME, 2012).

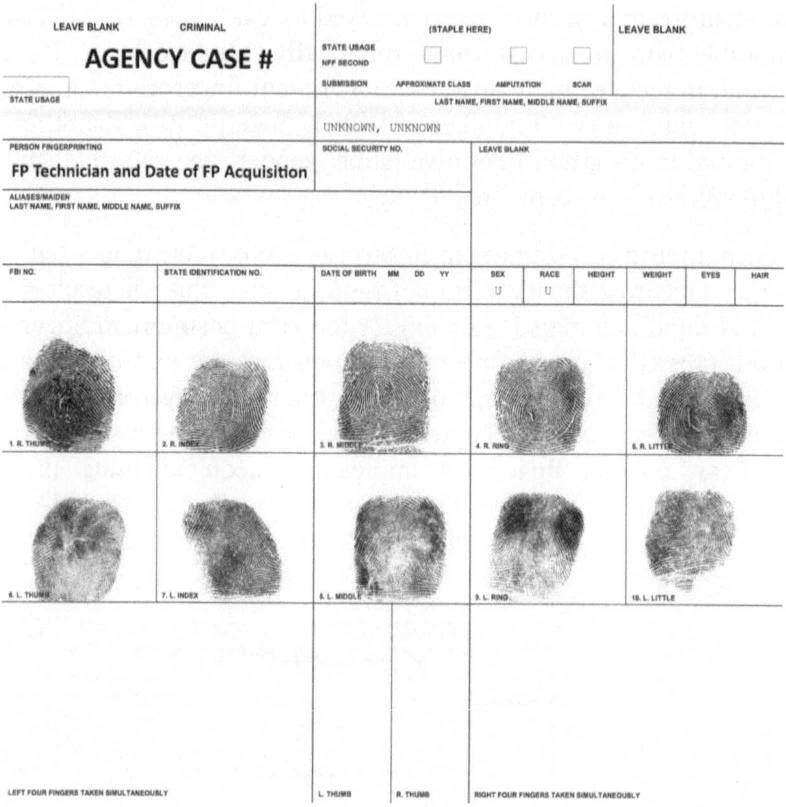

Figure 7.2c Ten-print fingerprint record acquired using the digital Livescan Technique (©NYC OCME, 2013).

Technique (Figure 7.2c), and/or Casting Technique (Figure 7.2d). Additionally, photographs of fingerprint castings with a scale can be imported into a digital ten-print fingerprint card (Figure 7.2e). Furthermore, photographs of epidermal friction ridge skin or fingers with a scale can be converted into negative impressions (since they are positive impressions) and imported into a digital ten-print fingerprint card. In the event of negative results during a ten-print automated fingerprint search of the unidentified postmortem fingerprint record, a more detailed, latent-fingerprint search should still be performed due to the lower examination-quality of postmortem fingerprint impressions. This will ensure that all attempts at fingerprint identification have been made.

Due to the varying conditions and decomposing stages of postmortem remains, latent fingerprint acquisition may be the only possibility. Postmortem latent fingerprints include photographs of fingerprint

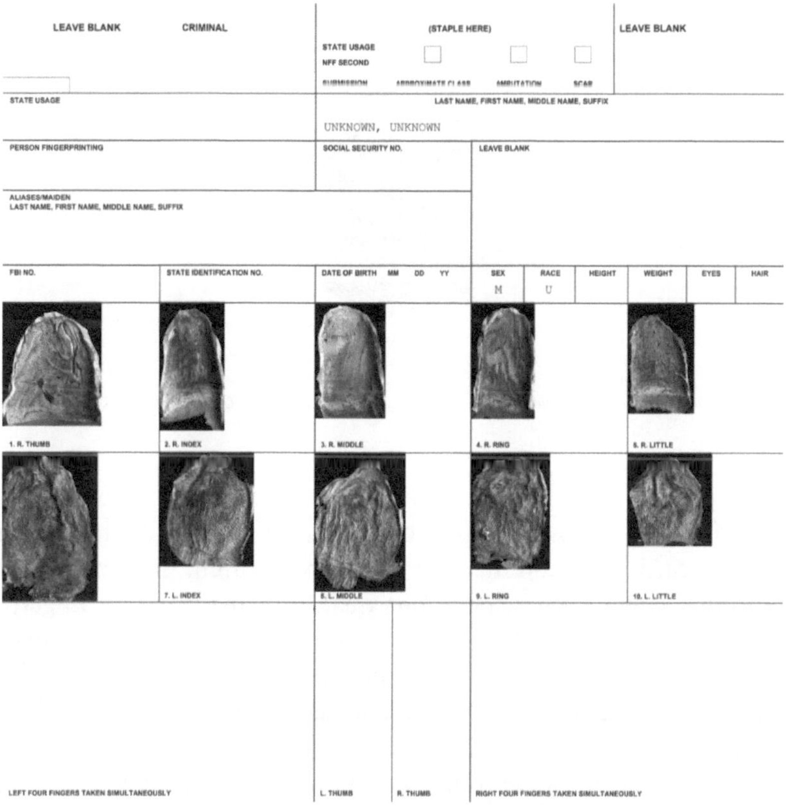
LEAVE BLANK CRIMINAL
(STAPLE HERE)
STATE USAGE
NFF SECOND
SUBMISSION APPROXIMATE CLASS AMPUTATION SCAR
LEAVE BLANK
STATE USAGE
LAST NAME, FIRST NAME, MIDDLE NAME, SUFFIX
UNKNOWN, UNKNOWN
PERSON FINGERPRINTING
SOCIAL SECURITY NO.
LEAVE BLANK
ALIASES/MAIDEN
LAST NAME, FIRST NAME, MIDDLE NAME, SUFFIX
FBI NO.
STATE IDENTIFICATION NO.
DATE OF BIRTH MM DD YY
SEX M
RACE U
HEIGHT
WEIGHT
EYES
HAIR
1. R. THUMB
2. R. INDEX
3. R. MIDDLE
4. R. RING
5. R. LITTLE
7. L. INDEX
8. L. MIDDLE
9. L. RING
10. L. LITTLE
LEFT FOUR FINGERS TAKEN SIMULTANEOUSLY
L. THUMB
R. THUMB
RIGHT FOUR FINGERS TAKEN SIMULTANEOUSLY

Figure 7.2d Ten-print fingerprint record acquired using the Casting Technique (©NYC OCME, 2012).

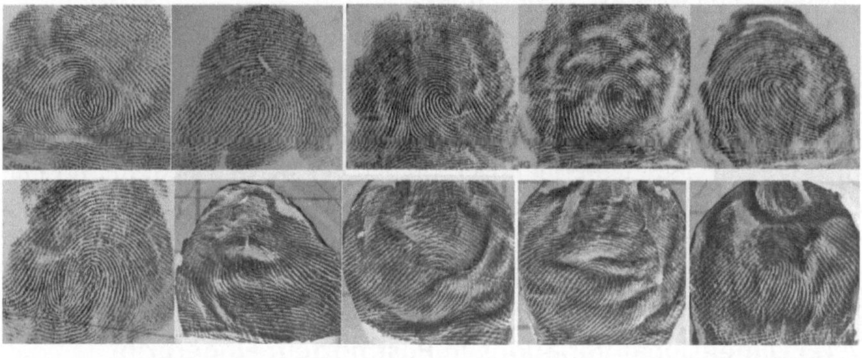

Figure 7.2e Ten-print fingerprint record created by importing individual photographs into a digital fingerprint card (©NYC OCME, 2013).

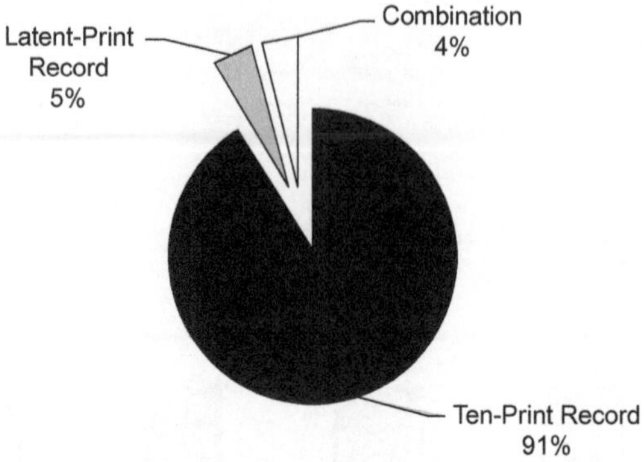

Figure 7.3 Use and frequency of acquisition media on 172 cases at the NYC OCME (Mulawka, Mosco, Uhle & Mokleby, 2013).

castings, photographs of epidermal friction ridge skin, or photographs of fingers. If these images cannot be imported into a digital ten-print fingerprint card and submitted for a ten-print search, they must be submitted for a latent-print search. The quality of the resulting fingerprint impressions may be very low, and because a latent-print search involves manual marking by a fingerprint examiner, the process is somewhat subjective. Another latent fingerprint examiner may mark the fingerprint in a different way due to experience, training, etc. As such, if a latent fingerprint search yields negative results when an unidentified postmortem fingerprint record is submitted, the record should be periodically searched. Multiple searches by different latent fingerprint examiners can increase the chances of identification, especially if the fingerprint record submitted for searching is of low examination-quality. This will ensure thorough attempts at fingerprint identification.

In a 2013 analysis of 172 postmortem fingerprint cases requiring fingerprint acquisition at the New York City Office of Chief Medical Examiner, the frequency of fingerprint acquisition media was observed (Figure 7.3). In 91% of all cases, ten-print fingerprint records were created. In 5% of all cases, only latent fingerprint records were created. A combination of both ten-print fingerprint records and latent fingerprint records was used in 4% of all cases (Mulawka et al., 2013).

7.1.6 Dimensional Variations in Postmortem Fingerprint Impressions

An important issue discovered in searches of unidentified postmortem fingerprint records is the dimensional variation associated with recovered postmortem impressions. Due to the varying condition of postmortem remains, the friction ridge skin may expand or shrink, which causes enlargement or reduction in the pattern area of the fingers. The size difference can significantly affect the accuracy of fingerprint-matching algorithms in AFIS, and therefore must be corrected by a fingerprint examiner through the use of size-scaling algorithms or digital imaging software prior to conducting an automated search (Uhle, 2007 and 2010). The dermal impressions from boiled or charred friction ridge skin may be significantly smaller than their matching antemortem epidermal fingerprint impressions (Figure 7.4). Conversely, the epidermal impressions from injected or degloved friction ridge skin may be significantly larger than their matching antemortem epidermal fingerprint

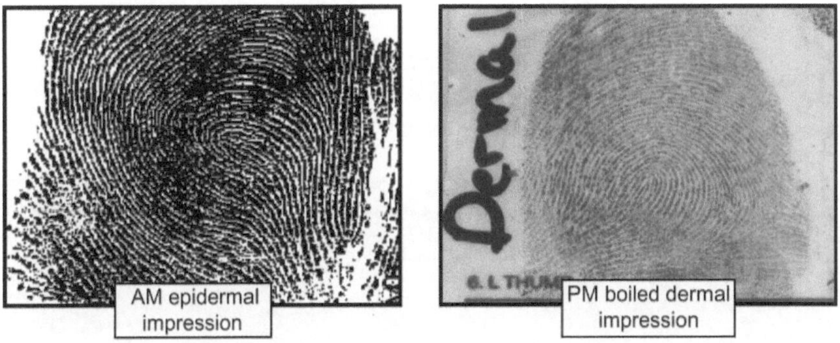

Figure 7.4 Epidermal antemortem fingerprint impression and corresponding boiled dermal fingerprint impression (©NYC OCME, 2012).

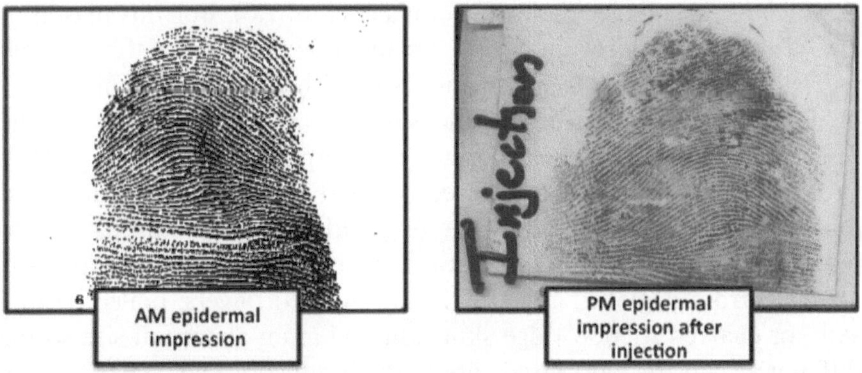

Figure 7.5a Epidermal antemortem fingerprint impression and corresponding epidermal fingerprint impression after injection (©NYC OCME, 2012).

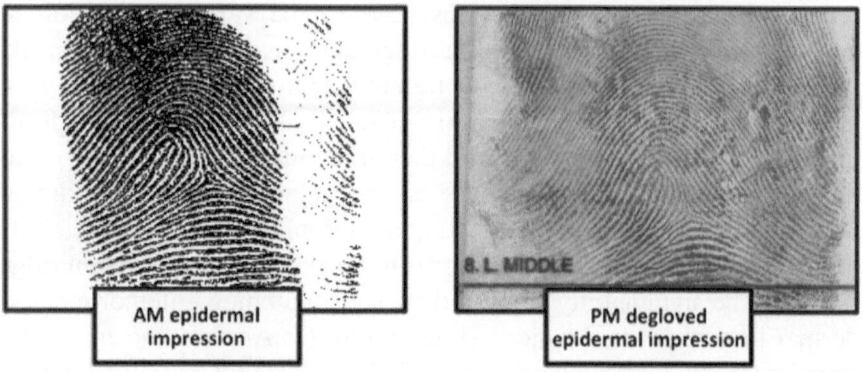

Figure 7.5b Epidermal antemortem fingerprint impression and corresponding degloved epidermal fingerprint impression (©NYC OCME, 2012).

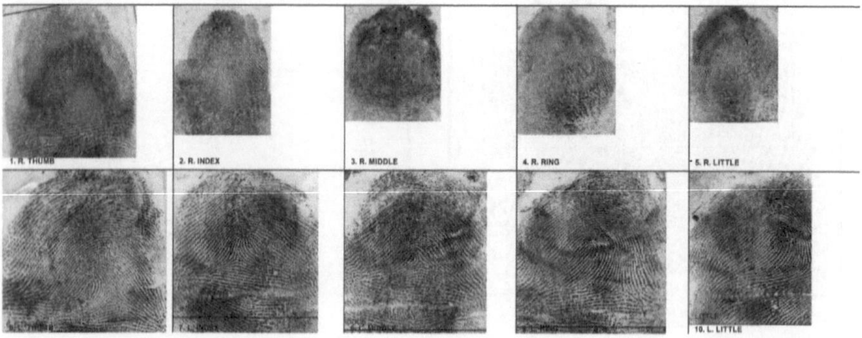

Figure 7.6 Fingerprint record exhibiting dermal fingerprint impressions (right) and degloved epidermal fingerprint impressions (left) (©NYC OCME, 2013).

impressions (Figure 7.5a,b). The epidermis from degloved skin can be as much as 33% larger than the dermis (Figure 7.6). For this reason, if an AFIS search does not reveal an identification using the original recording, the fingerprint impression should be searched again at 70% of its original size, or searched at over 100% of its original size if the fingerprint impressions are dermal (Fingerprint Sourcebook, 2010). Furthermore, it is imperative to record what techniques are being used during fingerprint acquisition. The fingerprint examiner that is searching the fingerprint record must know if a fingerprint impression was acquired from degloved epidermal skin, injected fingers, boiled dermal skin, or charred friction ridge skin resulting in an abnormal size so the difference can be addressed prior to conducting an AFIS search (Nursall, 2011).

7.2 INVESTIGATIVE TECHNIQUES USED TO LOCATE ANTEMORTEM FINGERPRINT RECORDS

It is important to know what information to look for when investigating information regarding location of antemortem fingerprint records. Just because an individual was fingerprinted at some point in their lifetime, it does not mean the fingerprint record exists or resides in a searchable database. If this is the case, the record will need to be located and requested. Location of the fingerprint record may involve research, outreach, and sending a formal fingerprint record request to the agency in possession of the desired antemortem fingerprint record. The agency in possession of the antemortem fingerprint record may refuse to release the information (some agencies are restricted from releasing fingerprint records by legislation). In this case, the agency in possession of the postmortem fingerprint record may have to provide the postmortem record to the other agency and request a fingerprint comparison (*See Appendix for Records Request Template*).

In the event of a tentative identification, in which circumstantial information provides a missing person's name for the decedent, it is important to gather as much information as possible regarding the missing person. A thorough search of the death scene or tentative decedent's residence can reveal crucial information that will aid in antemortem fingerprint record location. Any documentation displaying antemortem fingerprint records should be photographed with a scale using the highest resolution possible, impounded, and transported back to the Medical Examiner/Coroner Office or law enforcement agency. If the item is not photographed at a high resolution, the document displaying the AM fingerprint record should be scanned on a high-resolution scanner (at least 500 dpi) and saved as a TIFF, JPEG 2000, or JPEG image. Additionally, any documentation from the scene that would imply that a fingerprint record may be available should be photographed and collected. If next-of-kin is available, an antemortem interview can facilitate narrowing down the search for antemortem fingerprint records. The questions in the table below can lead the investigator to possible sources that may lead to location of the missing person's antemortem fingerprint records.

Antemortem Fingerprint Investigation Questions
1. Was the individual ever fingerprinted for a job (teacher, lawyer, banker, etc.)?
2. Was the individual ever fingerprinted for the government?
3. Was the individual ever in the military or reserves?

4. Was the individual ever fingerprinted for immigration purposes?
5. Was the individual ever fingerprinted for benefits (i.e. food stamps, public assistance, etc.)?
6. Was the individual ever fingerprinted for an arrest?
7. Did the individual ever have a State ID or DL in another state?
8. Was the individual ever fingerprinted for a bank account, gym membership, or other membership?
9. Was the individual ever fingerprinted for an association (i.e. American Bar Association, etc.)?
10. Was the individual ever fingerprinted for technology equipment access (i.e. smartphone, USB hard drive, computer log-in, etc.)?
11. Did the individual ever purchase fingerprint art or fingerprint jewelry?
12. Did the individual possess any documentation that contains fingerprint records?

7.3 SUBMISSION OF ANTEMORTEM AND POSTMORTEM FINGERPRINT RECORDS FOR DIRECT FINGERPRINT COMPARISONS

If an antemortem fingerprint record is located in the event of a tentative identification, the record must be compared to the postmortem fingerprint record. If the antemortem fingerprint record is a physical document, the document should be scanned on a high-resolution scanner (at least 500 dpi) and saved as a TIFF, JPEG 2000, or JPEG image. If an agency does not employ ten-print or latent fingerprint examiners, both records should be submitted to the nearest local or state law enforcement agency for comparison. In the event this is not possible, both fingerprint records can be submitted manually via email as a special request to the FBI CJIS SPC following the procedures delineated in the next section (7.4). If the antemortem fingerprint record, postmortem fingerprint record, or both records qualify as latent prints, a comparison request cannot be submitted to the FBI CJIS SPC. Instead, both fingerprint records should be submitted manually via email as a special request to the DHS BSC West Latent Print Unit following the procedures delineated in the last section (7.5). The fingerprint records can also be submitted manually to the FBI Laboratory Latent Operations Unit.

7.4 MANUAL SUBMISSION OF POSTMORTEM FINGERPRINT RECORDS TO THE FEDERAL BUREAU OF INVESTIGATION CRIMINAL JUSTICE INFORMATION SERVICES DIVISION SPECIAL PROCESSING CENTER (FBI CJIS SPC)

In an effort to aid in forensic identification of unidentified human remains, the Federal Bureau of Investigation Criminal Justice Information Services Division Special Processing Center (FBI CJIS SPC) assists non-law enforcement agencies with the searching of postmortem fingerprint records against IAFIS/NGI. If an agency does not possess AFIS terminals or have easy access to one, fingerprint records can be submitted manually via email or facsimile. The procedures below delineate directions for submitting fingerprints to the FBI CJIS SPC (Mulawka & Craig, 2011).

1. A template should be created to include the following information on a facsimile cover sheet, email, or cover letter bearing the submitting agency's logo:

FBI CJIS SPC Submission Template Information
• Type of transaction—DEU (Unknown Deceased) • Submitting agency's name • Submitting agency's ORI number • Date and time of submission • Name of individual submitting the entry • Submitting agency's case number • Decedent's date of death • Decedent's possible name or aliases, date of birth, social security number • Decedent's demographics (male or female, race, approximate age, etc.) • Case synopsis and any other useful information • A request to ensure all available databases are searched (IAFIS/NGI criminal and civil, DHS IDENT, DoD ABIS, etc.) • A request to ensure the postmortem record is retained in the event of negative results • A request to be forwarded for a latent print search in the event of negative results during ten-print search • Special acquisition techniques used that may affect the AFIS search

See Appendix for FBI CJIS SPC Fingerprint Submission Form Template

2. The original postmortem fingerprint card should be examined and, depending on the quality of the fingerprints, a mode of transmission should be decided (facsimile or email).
3. Copies of the postmortem fingerprint record(s) and enlargements (130% and 150%) should be made if faxing the record. If emailing the record, the card should be scanned on a flatbed scanner at minimum 500 d.p.i. and saved in TIFF format (preferred, but JPEG, JPEG 2000, and PDF are also acceptable). If multiple original fingerprint cards are available, at least two or three fingerprint cards can be included in the submission depending on the quality of the fingerprints.
4. All information (facsimile cover sheet, 100% photocopy, 130% enlargement, 150% enlargement) should be submitted using superfine or ultrafine settings when submitting via facsimile.

5. All information [cover letter information, digital TIFF (or other accepted format) file(s)] should be submitted with attachments included when submitting via email. The total size of the attachments cannot exceed 10MB. If the size exceeds 10MB, the email will not go through and will be returned. If there are multiple attachments under 10MB each, multiple emails can be sent with each separate attachment.
6. Once the emailed or faxed information goes through, the fax receipt or email receipt should be stored with the electronic case file for record-keeping purposes.
7. A follow-up phone call should be made to FBI CJIS SPC to ensure there were no issues with the transmission.
8. After the record is searched, FBI CJIS SPC will send results via facsimile; this documentation should be stored with the electronic case file for record-keeping purposes.

FBI CJIS SPC Contact Information
FBI CJIS Special Processing Center 1000 Custer Hollow Road, Module E2 Clarksburg, WV 26306 304-625-5584 phone 304-625-5587 fax **spc@leo.gov**

If FBI CJIS SPC fingerprint examiners have any issue with the submission, a phone call or facsimile will be received stating the issue and suggestions for resubmission. In the event of negative results following an unidentified postmortem fingerprint submission, the FBI CJIS SPC has the ability to enter the unidentified postmortem fingerprints into IAFIS/NGI for retention, assigning the record with a specific FBI number, and conducting periodic searches against uploaded antemortem records. However, when fingerprints are emailed or faxed to the FBI CJIS SPC, they cannot be assigned an FBI number because the fingerprint search being performed is a courtesy search. In order to retain and/or update a fingerprint record, the fingerprint record must be submitted to the agency's state fingerprint bureau, which will then electronically forward the fingerprint record to the FBI CJIS SPC. Once received, a unique FBI number will be assigned to the unidentified postmortem fingerprint record and the record will be retained in IAFIS/NGI. A confirmation is sent back to the state bureau listing the new FBI number assigned and the state bureau will in turn notify the contributing agency. If a fingerprint record is resubmitted to the FBI CJIS SPC and it already resides as an unidentified postmortem fingerprint record, it will be matched to the previously submitted record and associated FBI number.

7.5 MANUAL SUBMISSION OF POSTMORTEM FINGERPRINT RECORDS TO THE DEPARTMENT OF HOMELAND SECURITY BIOMETRIC SUPPORT CENTER (DHS BSC)

In an effort to aid with forensic identification of unidentified human remains, the Department of Homeland Security Biometric Support Center assists non-law enforcement agencies with the searching of postmortem fingerprint records against IDENT. Fingerprint records can be submitted manually via email or facsimile. The procedures below delineate directions on submitting fingerprints to the DHS BSC (Mulawka & Craig, 2011).

1. A current DHS BSC Fingerprint Submission Form should be obtained from DHS BSC (currently hard and electronic copies are available) and the appropriate information should be populated on the form.
2. A template should be created to include the following information on a facsimile cover sheet, email, or cover letter bearing the submitting agency's logo:

DHS BSC Submission Template Information
• Type of transaction—DEU (Unknown Deceased) • Submitting agency's name • Submitting agency's ORI number • Date and time of submission • Name of individual submitting the entry • Submitting agency's case number • Decedent's date of death • Decedent's possible name or aliases, date of birth, social security number • Decedent's demographics (male or female, race, approximate age, etc.) • Case synopsis and any other useful information • A request to ensure all available databases are searched (DHS IDENT, IAFIS/NGI criminal and civil, INTERPOL, etc.) • A request to be forwarded for a latent print search in the event of negative results during ten-print search • Special acquisition techniques used that may affect the AFIS search

See Appendix for DHS BSC Fingerprint Submission Form Template

3. The original postmortem fingerprint card should be examined and, depending on the quality of the fingerprints, a mode of transmission should be decided (facsimile or email).

4. Copies of the postmortem fingerprint record(s) and enlargements (130% and 150%) should be made if faxing the record. If emailing the record, the card should be scanned on a flatbed scanner at minimum 500 d.p.i. and saved in TIFF format (preferred, but JPEG, JPEG 2000, and PDF are also acceptable). If multiple original fingerprint cards are available, at least two or three fingerprint cards can be included in the submission depending on the quality of the fingerprints.
5. All information (fax cover sheet, 100% photocopy, 130% enlargement, 150% enlargement) should be submitted using superfine or ultrafine settings when submitting via facsimile.
6. All information [DHS BSC Fingerprint Submission Form, cover letter information, digital TIFF (or other accepted format) file(s)] should be submitted with attachments when submitting via email. The total size of the attachments cannot exceed 10MB. If the size exceeds 10MB, the email will not go through and will be returned. If there are multiple attachments under 10MB each, multiple emails can be sent with each separate attachment.
7. Once the emailed or faxed information goes through, the fax receipt or email receipt should be stored with the electronic case file for record-keeping purposes.
8. A follow-up phone call should be made to DHS BSC to ensure there were no issues with the transmission.
9. After the record is searched, DHS BSC will send results via facsimile; this documentation should be stored with the electronic case file for record-keeping purposes.

DHS BSC Contact Information
DHS BSC West 9275 Sky Park Court San Diego, CA 92123 858-609-2609 phone 858-609-2600 fax **afis@dhs.gov** (ten print) **lpu@dhs.gov** (latent print) DHS BSC East 1616 North Fort Myer Drive Suite 1800 Arlington, VA 22209 202-298-5199 phone

CHAPTER 8

Postmortem Fingerprint Record Case Management

Due to the complexity of various aspects pertaining to postmortem fingerprint identification delineated in this book—postmortem fingerprint recovery, antemortem fingerprint record investigation, submission procedures to multiple agencies, cold case resubmission procedures to multiple agencies, fingerprint record identification, fingerprinting during mass fatality incidents, statistical gathering, and research—postmortem fingerprint record case management can be overwhelming. Before an agency makes the decision to develop a postmortem fingerprinting initiative, a consistent process and workflow must be established to maintain proper documentation, chain of custody, quality assurance, quality control, and ensure the initiative's success. Furthermore, with the advancement of technology and conversion of all records into digital form, it is imperative to configure an electronic case management system or database to suit a specific agency's needs for adequate fingerprint record case management.

8.1 ESTABLISHING POSTMORTEM FINGERPRINT OPERATIONS POLICIES, PROTOCOLS, AND STANDARD OPERATING PROCEDURES

When developing a postmortem fingerprinting initiative, an agency should thoroughly research corresponding local, state, and federal legislation regarding unidentified human remains and fingerprint submissions. Once this information is learned the agency should perform outreach and develop points of contact with any external agencies that will be directly or indirectly involved with postmortem fingerprint records or corresponding information. Often, memorandums of agreement are required for some agencies, as well as policy or workflow changes that can take a significant amount of time. Without these changes, there may be major internal fingerprint workflow issues that can impact a forensic agency's overall identification operations.

Consequently, identifications may be delayed and may, in turn, lead to potential unforeseen legal ramifications.

Researching available grants is also beneficial, as funding may be available through the National Institute of Justice (NIJ) or other federal, state, and local resources. The agency should establish a specific budget for fingerprint supplies, equipment, equipment maintenance, personnel, training, continuing education, and research (Figure 8.1a–f). Proper resource allocation must be considered regarding full-time, part-time, or grant-funded staff. At least one person must be designated as the major point of contact and manager of all fingerprint-related operations. In a large agency with a high caseload, another individual should be designated to coordinate ongoing operations, statistics, trainings, continuing education, conferences, research, etc. Additionally, specific staff should be trained as fingerprint technicians, receiving adequate training in basic and advanced postmortem fingerprint recovery techniques (described in detail in Chapters 3 and 4). As postmortem fingerprint

Figure 8.1a–f Fingerprint supplies, personnel, and equipment (©NYC OCME 2012–2013).

recovery can be very complex and fingerprint identification is designated as a scientific identification modality, all fingerprint technicians should possess a scientific background and adequate training. It should be noted that training in advanced postmortem fingerprint recovery techniques is significantly extensive and will require time, supplies, and funding. It is also beneficial for fingerprint technicians to receive training in ten- and latent-fingerprint fundamentals, as grasping these concepts will aid in obtaining higher examination-quality fingerprint records. Furthermore, resources and personnel must be allocated for administrative tasks, investigation of antemortem fingerprint records, case follow-up, case review, and cold case responsibilities. As fingerprint techniques and technologies are constantly advancing, funding should also be allocated for ongoing continuing education and supplemental training.

Internal identification policies should be reviewed and any changes in fingerprint workflow must be incorporated into the overall agency policies and procedures. Protocols must be developed for overall fingerprint operations and Standard Operating Procedures (SOPs) must be written for the scientific techniques being used in order to ensure consistency, chain of custody, quality assurance, and quality control. All documentation should be reviewed and signed off on by agency management and any revisions should also be documented. If the agency houses any other scientific departments, such as DNA, anthropology, toxicology, etc., the other departments should be consulted with in the event that any other policies must change as a result of fingerprint operations. Identification, pathology, and medicolegal investigation divisions should also be consulted with for policy or procedural changes. Any documentation produced for fingerprint operations should follow a similar format to the other units in order to maintain consistency agency-wide. Lastly, due to the advancement in digital fingerprint technology, the agency must work very closely with its information technology (IT) department, as it will be significantly involved with many aspects of fingerprint operations.

A fingerprint wet lab or designated area must also be established for any postmortem fingerprint recovery operations, photography, scanning, and storage of biohazardous fingerprint cards. This area can also be used for storage of supplies, equipment, and fingerprinting kits described in Chapters 3 and 4. The agency should also establish a separate clean office area for administrative tasks, non-biohazardous record storage, etc. A separate mailbox, email address, phone number, and fax number for fingerprint operations should be created. A digital fax connected to the email address will allow all information to be sent to one inbox.

8.2 INTERNAL CASE MANAGEMENT SYSTEM OR DATABASE

After establishing a foundation for overall fingerprint operations delineated in the previous section, the next step is to create an electronic workflow and repository for all information relating to fingerprint operations. If the agency already utilizes an internal case management system, the information technology department and/or vendor should be consulted with prior to starting fingerprint operations. A separate drive must be established on the agency's internal network, as well as a separate section in the internal case management system. If the electronic case management system stores information for each separate case, all fingerprint information should be uploaded to the corresponding electronic case file.

In the event an agency does not have an internal case management system, fingerprint information and records can be managed using a database management program that can be configured to fit the agency's needs. Electronic case folders should be created on the network drive to organize all documents pertaining to fingerprint operations cases according to the steps in the fingerprint operations process they are in. Some examples include:

Fingerprint Operations Case Folder Examples
• Pending fingerprint acquisition (basic, advanced, photography) • Pending ten-print submissions (separated by agency) • Pending latent fingerprint submissions (separated by agency) • Identified via fingerprints (separated by agency that made identification) • Identified by other means (separated by modality)

8.3 STANDARD FORMS AND TEMPLATES

In order to maintain proper documentation and chain of custody, standard forms and templates should be created to document specific steps in the fingerprint identification process. It is best to keep all forms electronic, or scan paper-based forms into electronic form once they are completed. Forms and templates will document the fingerprint operations process, including postmortem fingerprint recovery techniques, submissions, and what work has been done on each case. Some examples include:

Fingerprint Operations Form and Template Examples
• Current Case Fingerprint Checklist: a chronologic checklist of responsibilities for a current fingerprint case • Cold Case Fingerprint Checklist: a chronologic checklist of responsibilities for a cold fingerprint case • Acquisition Form Templates: serves to document pertinent information and techniques used to acquire postmortem fingerprint records and supplements the fingerprint card • Submission Form Templates: serves to document pertinent information related to case, fingerprint submission, and supplements the fingerprint card • Records Request Templates: serves to document pertinent information related to case and requests an external agency to supply antemortem fingerprint record that can aid in identification

8.4 SPREADSHEET OR DATABASE OF FINGERPRINT OPERATIONS STATISTICS

Keeping track of statistics is important for any initiative or project, as it displays success or failure and can affect the project's continuation. Additionally, statistics help dictate policies, budgets, grant-funding, allocation of resources and supplies, research, and can serve to educate forensic professionals if trends are observed. As such, the collection of statistics pertaining to fingerprint operations is another important administrative aspect that an agency must plan for. Some examples of statistics to consider collecting include:

Fingerprint Operations Statistic Examples
• Total cases requiring fingerprint recovery (cases successfully printed, cases that had to be reprinted, cases that were designated as unprintable, etc.) • Total cases designated for fingerprint recovery, but identified via other modalities • Total cases designated for fingerprint recovery and identified via fingerprints (separated by agency, civil or criminal database, ten- vs. latent-print searches) • Total cases submitted for fingerprint searches (cases submitted to each separate agency or database) • Total cases submitted for fingerprint comparisons (cases submitted to each separate agency or database) • Total cases submitted as unknowns vs. tentative identifications • Total cases manually acquired and cardscanned vs. electronically acquired via livescan • Total cases requiring basic postmortem fingerprint recovery techniques (separated by type of basic technique) • Total cases requiring advanced postmortem fingerprint recovery techniques (separated by type of advanced technique) • Total cases acquired as ten-prints vs. latent-prints vs. both • Total cases acquired using epidermal skin vs. dermal skin vs. both • Total cold cases designated for resubmission • Total cold cases identified after resubmission (separated by agency, civil or criminal database, ten- vs. latent-print searches) • Total cold cases with negative results requiring future resubmissions

CHAPTER 9

Cold Case Unidentified Postmortem Fingerprint Records

The definition of a cold case varies between different agencies. The National Institute of Justice (NIJ) currently defines a cold case as "any case whose probative investigative leads have been exhausted" (Heurich, 2008). An unsolved case involving unidentified human remains that may only be a few months old may have turned "cold" if there are no more investigative leads available to follow. The emergence of new technologies allows the possibility of re-evaluating cold cases. New scientific techniques and technology may reveal new information that can aid in the cold case investigation. Officials can test samples that were unable to be examined in the past, or search larger repositories that were previously unavailable to identify cold cases that have been lying dormant for years and provide resolution to the victims' families.

9.1 COLD CASE INVESTIGATION IN THE UNITED STATES

Chapter 1 presents an overview of Unidentified Human Remains in the United States, emphasizing the enormous volume of unidentified and missing person cases that continue to accumulate with the passage of time, referred to as a "silent mass disaster over time" (Ritter, 2007). As a result of limited resources and knowledge of techniques in forensic identification and investigation, many of these cases have transitioned into cold cases. In order to address this issue, the NIJ has made federal resources available for state and local jurisdictions tasked with forensic identification to identify unidentified human remains and help solve missing persons cases.

The NIJ gathered forensic science and criminal justice experts to aid in developing a multifaceted plan that would address many of the gaps in forensic identifications across the United States. As part of the President's multi-year initiative to maximize the use of forensic DNA in solving crime, programs were created to train the forensic science and law enforcement communities on forensic DNA evidence, provide free DNA testing of human remains and family reference samples, and encourage jurisdictions to collect DNA samples and analyze old biological samples. Additionally, the NIJ has instituted programs to increase Medical Examiner/Coroner (ME/C) Office and Law Enforcement Agency (LEA) access and use of federal databases to link missing persons and unidentified human remains cases.

Due to the issues with unidentified and missing persons described in Chapter 1, the NIJ developed and instituted another major program known as the National Missing and Unidentified Persons System (NamUs), described in further detail in Chapter 6. NamUs is the first national repository for unidentified and missing persons information accessible online to ME/C offices, LEAs, and the public. The NamUs databases are one portion of a larger program to improve the nation's ability to address unidentified and missing persons cases. As a result of forming partnerships across the country, NamUs also provides free forensic services for agencies that may not have the resources, staff, and/or funding to access certain services. NamUs partnered with the University of North Texas Health Science Center for Human Identification (UNTCHI) to provide free DNA and anthropological testing. Local and state ME/C offices and LEAs can have free nuclear and mitochondrial DNA testing performed on unidentified human remains, missing persons reference samples, and family reference samples, which can then be added to the corresponding NamUs records. UNTCHI also provides free anthropological examinations on unidentified human remains to determine manner and cause of death. Furthermore, NamUs staff facilitates fingerprint database searches and fingerprint comparisons of unidentified postmortem fingerprint records.

Using the multitude of programs and funding made available by the NIJ, many local and state jurisdictions are able to identify, review, and investigate cold cases. As a result, many ME/C Offices, LEAs, and crime laboratories across the United States have established cold case units specifically dedicated to reviewing old cases. Many ME/Cs and LEAs have already been able to solve cases for missing and unidentified persons that have been unidentified for years. Efforts to solve these cases are becoming more thorough, advanced, and streamlined.

9.2 RESEARCH SUPPORTING COLD CASE POSTMORTEM FINGERPRINT RECORD RESUBMISSION

In 2004, the Bureau of Justice Statistics estimated that over half of the ME/C offices in the United States did not enforce policies on retaining records on UHR prior to disposition and burial (Hickman & Hughes, 2007). X-rays, DNA, or fingerprints were not retained from many of these cases and countless numbers of unidentified human remains were buried or cremated. Without the retention of these records, which can be used for further testing, the chances of identifying these individuals were severely diminished, if not eradicated (Mulawka *et al.*, 2010).

In 2007, procedures were created for the submission of unidentified postmortem fingerprint records to multiple local, state, and federal agencies at the San Diego County Medical Examiner's Office. Prior to these procedures, unidentified postmortem fingerprints were generally submitted only to the San Diego Sheriff's Office Cal-ID Fingerprint Division, a local fingerprint database. Starting in 2007, all legible unidentified postmortem fingerprint records at SDMEO from 1979 to 2009 cases were submitted to the Department of Homeland Security Biometric Support Center West (DHS BSC West) and the Federal Bureau of Investigation Criminal Justice Information Services Special Processing Center (FBI CJIS SPC), following the newly developed procedures, to determine whether a significant number of additional identifications would occur from this effort. Out of 109 cases, fifty-one persons (47%) were identified as a direct result of this study, including several cold cases dating back as far as 1979 (Mulawka & Craig, 2011). Since this study, other agencies have resubmitted cold case fingerprint records that were subsequently identified. Additionally, this study is used as an example in NamUs trainings and continuing education, which underlines "it is not sufficient to have your unidentified remains prints run only through your local or state fingerprint databases" (2012).

Mulawka and Craig's study supports the notion that potential fingerprint identifications have been missed by ME/Cs and LEAs throughout the nation due to a lack of knowledge regarding the fingerprint databases available and accessible to them for the humanitarian purpose of human forensic identification. If the ME/C, LEA, and forensic communities can better understand the strengths and limitations of current fingerprint technology and take measures to increase their federal submission capabilities, the probability of fingerprint identifications has the potential to increase on a nationwide scale. The location and periodic resubmission of all cold case postmortem fingerprint records is imperative due to continued advancement in fingerprint technology, increased interoperability, and retention inconsistencies.

9.3 REASONS FOR COLD CASE POSTMORTEM FINGERPRINT RECORD RESUBMISSION

As Automated Fingerprint Identification System (AFIS) technology advances (described detail in Chapter 7), more local, state, and federal jurisdictions will convert their antemortem fingerprint records into a digital format. As more records are uploaded into the agency's local AFIS, more fingerprint records populate the corresponding state bureau's repository and are forwarded to the FBI Integrated Automated Fingerprint Identification System/Next Generation Identification (IAFIS/NGI). As a result, a local jurisdiction in California may now have access to newly uploaded criminal fingerprint records from a local jurisdiction in New York through IAFIS/NGI. Additionally, interoperability is continually increasing between local, state, and federal databases (described detail in Chapter 6). Some agencies are now receiving fingerprint record uploads from other repositories due to established memorandums of agreement. A local jurisdiction in Nevada may now have access to newly uploaded civil fingerprint records from a local jurisdiction in Utah. Furthermore, AFIS searching algorithms are continuously advancing, increasing the probability of fingerprint identifications. Between the years 2011–2012, the New York City Police Department, New York State Division of Criminal Justice Services (NYS DCJS), and the Federal Bureau of Investigation Criminal Justice Information Services Division upgraded their respective Automated Fingerprint Identification Systems. The NYS DCJS upgraded their SAFIS to SABIS and the FBI is in the incremental process of transitioning IAFIS into NGI. These system upgrades also included enhancements of more advanced fingerprint-matching algorithms for ten- and latent-fingerprint searches, resulting in a significantly increased probability of fingerprint identification.

Another major issue with unidentified postmortem fingerprint records is that of retention. The FBI IAFIS/NGI will retain the unidentified record indefinitely if the record is submitted through the originating agency's state bureau as a Deceased Unknown (DEU) Transaction type (Chapter 7). However, local and state agencies may have different retention policies and may expunge the unidentified postmortem record after a certain time period. Thus, a postmortem fingerprint record that was previously searched and yielded negative results should be resubmitted periodically for searching again against all available local, state, and federal antemortem fingerprint records.

Finally, due to the subjectivity of latent fingerprint searching and dimensional variations in postmortem fingerprint impressions described in Chapter 7, a new latent-print search should be conducted in the event of negative ten-print searching results following cold case postmortem fingerprint resubmission. A different latent fingerprint examiner may manually encode the fingerprint differently than the previous latent fingerprint examiner; the examiner may also have updated and more advanced training. Advancement in latent-print searching algorithms further increases the chance of identification following resubmission.

9.4 ESTABLISHMENT OF A COLD CASE FINGERPRINT PROJECT

If an agency has established a Cold Case Unit or Task Force, it should create a Cold Case Fingerprint Project. All cold case postmortem fingerprint records should be located, inventoried, assessed, and scanned into electronic format. Depending on the agency's AFIS terminal access and fingerprint submission procedures, an FBI-approved cardscan (online scanner) can be used to scan and convert any manually acquired fingerprint records into the ANSI/NIST standard and EBTS-compliant format, which will allow for the electronic fingerprint transmission and subsequent searches of the local, state, and FBI IAFIS/NGI via a secure line connection (Chapter 7).

The record will still have to be manually searched against other databases that are not accessible electronically, such as DHS or other surrounding state and federal bureaus. These other agencies, described in Chapter 6, may require a more compatible format, such as JPEG, JPEG 2000, TIFF, or PDF files. Once the electronic record is created, it should be stored in an internal case management system or database (Chapter 8) and searched against all available fingerprint databases. The Postmortem Fingerprint Submission Strategy and procedures described in Chapter 7 should be followed to resubmit records to the appropriate local, state, federal, and international agencies in order to perform an adequate and thorough search of all available fingerprint records (Figure 7.1).

In the event that a jurisdiction has a large amount of cold case unidentified fingerprint records and limited resources, NamUs can be contacted for assistance. Additionally, the jurisdiction can contact the Federal Bureau of Investigation Criminal Justice Information Services Special Processing Center (FBI CJIS SPC) and Department of Homeland Security Biometric Support Center directly to discuss submitting the unidentified postmortem fingerprint records in batches. Furthermore, the FBI CJIS has a special Flyaway Program that can assist with conducting ten- and latent-fingerprint searches of IAFIS/NGI on site at any domestic location and can be requested by state and local agencies (Chapter 10).

9.5 COLD CASE POSTMORTEM FINGERPRINT RECOVERY

A significant fallback with cold case postmortem fingerprint identification may be that examination-quality fingerprint impressions and the remains may not be available anymore to attempt new postmortem fingerprint recovery. Current advanced postmortem fingerprint recovery techniques may not have been available at the time of acquisition and as a result, the only impressions available may be of very low examination-quality. In these cases, it is best to scan the original fingerprint card at the highest resolution available. If the body is available or exhumed for DNA acquisition purposes, another attempt at postmortem friction ridge recovery should be attempted using the techniques described in Chapters 3 and 4 (Figure 9.1a,b).

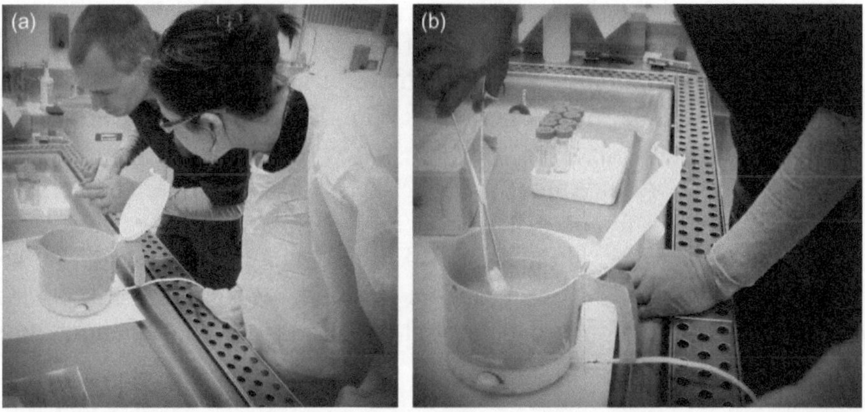

Figure 9.1a,b Use of Boiling Technique following Rehydration Technique on exhumed cold case (©NYC OCME 2012).

CHAPTER 10

Postmortem Fingerprint Recovery During Mass Fatality Incidents

A Mass Fatality Incident (MFI) can occur anywhere and at any time; many can occur without advance warning. When MFIs occur, recovering and identifying human remains is a significant aspect of the response. The local Medical Examiner/Coroner Office is responsible for overseeing and coordinating recovery and identification of the deceased. Depending on the nature of the mass fatality incident, some victim identifications may be expedited by fingerprint identification. Advancements in automated fingerprint technology for fingerprint acquisition and searching has made fingerprint identification rapid and efficient during MFIs. Antemortem fingerprint repositories can be electronically searched and in some cases, trained personnel can collect latent footprints from personal effects, residences, or businesses of suspected victims (NIJ, 2005). It is important to ensure that personnel are trained in manual postmortem fingerprint recovery techniques and manual supplies are still available, as the MFI may have affected electronic and communication lines.

Remains that have been burned or have sustained significant trauma may be difficult to process for postmortem fingerprint recovery and involve time, supplies, resources, personnel, and advanced equipment. Due to the unforeseen nature and timing of MFIs, an agency should have a preset plan for fingerprint operations during an incident. The plan should contain a contact list of trained personnel available for conducting fingerprint operations, Standard Operating Procedures, a blueprint of the disaster morgue fingerprint station (Figure 10.1) with inventory of equipment and supplies, a list of all perishable supplies in the event an emergency order must be placed, and various templates for fingerprint submissions. An extra supply cache should be prepared and stored in an accessible location. Any mobile equipment dedicated for MFIs should be stored with the extra supply cache and be ready for deployment.

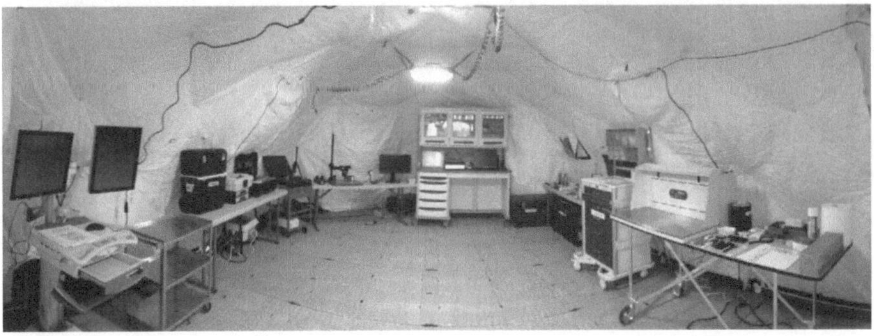

Figure 10.1 Mass fatality incident disaster morgue fingerprint station (©NYC OCME 2013).

10.1 FEDERAL BUREAU OF INVESTIGATION (FBI) DISASTER SQUAD AND FLYAWAY PROGRAM

If the magnitude of the MFI exceeds agency's local capabilities and its resources are too overwhelmed, additional resources, support, and personnel can be requested to assist with recovery operations, morgue operations, and identification operations. Depending on the nature of the incident, some agencies, such as the Federal Bureau of Investigation (FBI), respond immediately to provide support. The FBI has a Disaster Squad composed of a team of highly-trained forensic experts who can be immediately deployed worldwide to aid in victim identification during MFIs. The Disaster Squad consists of latent print examiners from the FBI Laboratory who are experts in the field of friction ridge analysis, as well as basic and advanced postmortem fingerprint recovery techniques. These forensic experts can aid in victim fingerprint identification through fingerprints, palm prints, and occasionally footprints.

Once postmortem fingerprint records are recovered, examiners can use mobile digital technology to perform on-site ten- and latent-print searches of postmortem fingerprint records against IAFIS/NGI. In the event that no identification is effected, records can also be submitted to other federal, state, and local agencies for automated searches in additional fingerprint databases. Furthermore, the FBI CJIS has a special Flyaway Program that can assist with conducting ten- and latent-fingerprint searches of IAFIS/NGI on site at any domestic location. The Flyaway Program services can be requested by local, state, federal, or international agencies and can deploy within four hours from notification. The Flyaway Team can also assist with ten- and latent-print searches of victim fingerprints (FBI, 2009 & 2010).

CHAPTER 11

Future Fingerprint Trends, Expectations, and Research

The rapid advancement of biometric and fingerprint technology is causing significant improvements in many aspects of fingerprint identification. Enhanced fingerprint matching algorithms for ten- and latent-fingerprint searches, increased repository size, and interoperability are all leading to a higher probability of positive fingerprint identifications. Additionally, biometric capture devices are becoming more mobile and streamlined. However, many of these advancements are occurring due to research for improving antemortem digital fingerprint capture. Research, development, and improvements in the area of postmortem fingerprint recovery, digital fingerprint capture, and fingerprint electronic processing is necessary. Furthermore a central fingerprint repository for retention of postmortem fingerprint records and missing person antemortem fingerprint records would considerably improve the identification of unidentified and missing persons.

11.1 FINGERPRINT TECHNOLOGY ADVANCEMENTS AND BIOMETRICS

Rapid advancement in Automated Fingerprint Identification System (AFIS) technology is causing significant improvements in speed, efficiency, convenience, accuracy, reliability, and affordability of fingerprint searches. The transition into multimodal biometrics allows for the digital capture of more information, such as multiple scans of the same finger for more thorough fingerprint matching. Other biometric modalities being used for identification and verification purposes include facial, voice, iris, and handwriting recognition. As such, local, state, and federal agencies with AFIS systems will be continuously upgrading current technology and transitioning to using Automated Biometric Identification Systems (ABIS).

The Federal Bureau of Investigation Criminal Justice Information Services Division established the Biometric Center of Excellence (BCOE) in 2007 to enhance current FBI biometric systems by exploring new biometric technologies. The BCOE also coordinates biometric advancement efforts, development, and research with local, state, and other federal agencies, as well as academic institutions and the private sector. Additionally, the BCOE is establishing biometric standards, certifying biometric products, and ensuring streamlined interoperability between current FBI biometric systems and other local, state, federal, and international biometric systems.

The FBI CJIS Division is currently upgrading the Integrated Automated Fingerprint Identification System (IAFIS) to Next Generation Identification (NGI) over a multi-year timespan in order to further advance biometric identification services. The NGI system implementation is an incremental replacement of the IAFIS and will provide state-of-the-art biometric identification services, advanced functionality, and enhancement of existing capabilities (described in detail in Chapter 6). This technology upgrade will accommodate increased biometric information processing and sharing demands from local, state, federal, and international agencies (FBI, 2009). The NGI Program will also allow non-law enforcement agencies, such as some Medical Examiner/Coroner Offices, to obtain an unrestricted Originating Agency Identification (ORI) Number that will allow access to the Interstate Identification Index (described detail in Chapter 7).

11.1.1 Increased Repository Size and Interoperability

As local, state, and federal jurisdictions will transition into using ABIS, biometric repositories will be populated with more records from all levels. Existing antemortem fingerprint records will be converted into digital format and any future antemortem records will be captured electronically using biometric devices. Additionally, interoperability is continually increasing between local, state, and federal databases (described in detail in Chapter 6). The FBI established the Biometric Interoperability Program to support local, state, and federal agencies in gaining access to expanded repositories for ten-print and latent fingerprint searches. In addition, more local and state agencies are continuing to establish memorandums of agreement with surrounding jurisdictions to exchange biometric repository and share information. As a result, jurisdictions on all levels will have access to more fingerprint records throughout the country.

11.1.2 Advanced Fingerprint-Matching Algorithms

ABIS technology will also increase in accuracy and daily fingerprint processing capacity due to more advanced matching algorithms. It will also significantly enhance current ten-print and latent fingerprint processing, allowing for more rapid results and increasing the probability of fingerprint identification. As this technology continues to advance, further research and development is required in current ten-print and latent fingerprint-matching algorithms to account for dimensional variations in postmortem fingerprint impressions (described detail in Chapter 7). Also, further research is warranted for the conversion of livescanned fingerprint castings (Figure 5.6 in Chapter 5).

11.1.3 Advancement in Biometric Capture Devices

Rapid advancements in fingerprint capture technology is causing significant improvements in mobility, speed, efficiency, accuracy, reliability, and affordability. Improvements are making digital fingerprint capture devices, or livescans, much more streamlined. Non-contact scanners are in development, which create a three-dimensional impression that will be converted to a two-dimensional impression for searching in current biometric repositories that contain two-dimensional fingerprint records (Liscio, 2013). Furthermore, current digital fingerprint capture devices were designed to record fingerprints from living subjects and are difficult to manipulate against decedents exhibiting rigor mortis and/or advanced postmortem changes (Figure 11.1) (explained in detail in Chapter 5). Placing deteriorating friction ridge detail on a platen and manipulating the fingers can further deteriorate the friction ridge detail. Further research and development is currently in process to produce devices that are specifically geared toward enhancing the postmortem fingerprint capture process, such as ruggedized, mobile, wireless, non-contact scanners. These "deadscan" devices will make the digital postmortem fingerprinting process less cumbersome and awkward. In addition, the non-contact scanners will be able to capture friction ridge detail that is within the depressions of desiccated and mummified fingers (Figure 11.2) or remains exhibiting advanced postmortem changes (Figure 11.3). As this technology continues to advance, further research and development is required in current ten-print and latent fingerprint-matching algorithms to account for dimensional variations in three-dimensional postmortem fingerprint impressions that are converted to two-dimensional postmortem fingerprint impressions. Additionally, further research is warranted for non-contact scanning of fingerprint castings, and resulting three- to two-dimensional conversions.

Another area of improvement for postmortem fingerprinting would be to streamline the current manual and cumbersome process of importing high-resolution photographs (with scale) of fingers, friction ridge skin, or castings into an electronic ten-print fingerprint card (described in detail in Chapter 4, Figure 4.9b). Cardscan software could be modified to automatically import each individual photograph

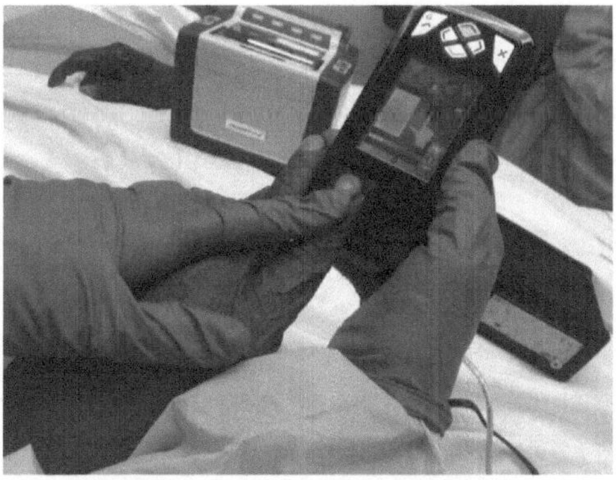

Figure 11.1 Postmortem fingerprint capture using mobile digital capture device (© NYC OCME 2012).

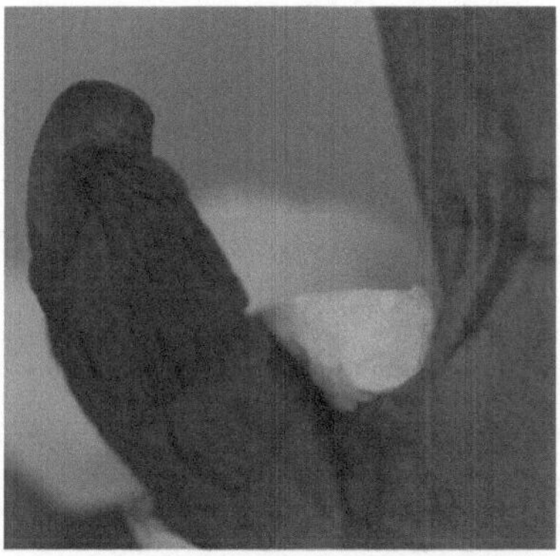

Figure 11.2 Depressions in postmortem friction ridge skin (©NYC OCME 2012).

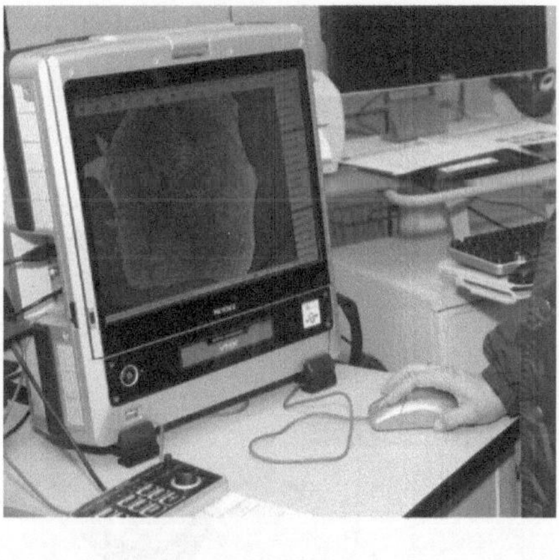

Figure 11.3 Enlargement of high-resolution photograph of fingerprint casting (©NYC OCME 2012).

into the corresponding fingerprint card block. In addition, if photographs of fingers or skin are to be imported, an automatic image reversal (creating a negative impression since photos of skin or fingers are positive impressions) should occur as well (Figure 11.3).

11.2 A UNIFORM FINGERPRINT REPOSITORY FOR UNIDENTIFIED AND MISSING PERSONS

Due to the issues and complexities involved in searching postmortem fingerprint records against various fingerprint repositories as described in Chapters 6 and 7, a uniform fingerprint repository for unidentified and missing persons should be incorporated into the new Next Generation Identification (NGI) system. This repository should be modeled after the Missing Persons and Unidentified Persons Indices of the Combined DNA Index System (CODIS), which is used to identify unidentified human remains by matching DNA profiles from unidentified human remains to DNA profiles of missing persons or their biological relatives. The indices are periodically searched against one another, as new DNA profiles are being uploaded daily. For fingerprint identification purposes, two indices should be created within NGI for the forensic identification of unidentified human remains for humanitarian purposes (Figure 11.4).

The Missing Persons Index (MPI) should be populated with antemortem fingerprint records from missing persons that have been authorized and uploaded from local, county, and state Medical Examiner/Coroner (ME/C) Offices and Law Enforcement Agencies (LEAs). When families of missing persons submit DNA reference samples, they sign a release form allowing the DNA profile to be searched against missing persons. The same type of authorization should be issued to families of missing

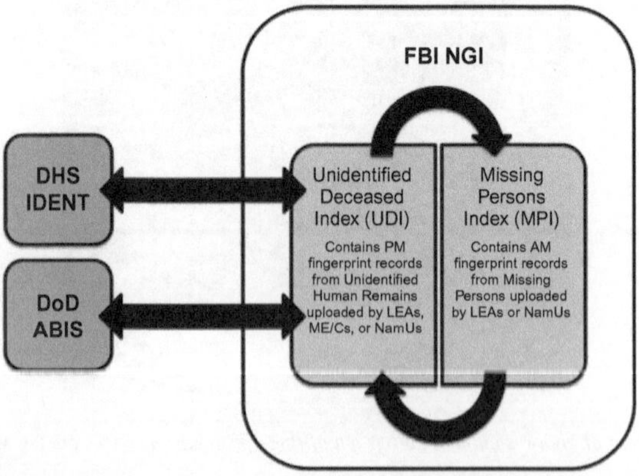

Figure 11.4 Schematic of uniform fingerprint repository for unidentified and missing persons.

persons that are providing the missing person's antemortem fingerprint records for upload to MPI. Once uploaded, a ten-print search of the antemortem fingerprint record should be performed against all available unidentified postmortem fingerprint records. In the event of negative results, a latent-print search of the antemortem fingerprint record should be performed against all available unidentified postmortem fingerprint records. In the event of negative ten- and latent-print searching results, the missing person antemortem fingerprint record should be retained indefinitely in MPI and continuously searched until the record is identified or removed upon request. The MPI will be restricted from searching against any other fingerprint indices, just as the family and direct reference sample indices are restricted from searching against any other databases in CODIS.

The Unidentified Deceased Index (UDI) should be populated with postmortem fingerprint records from decedents that have been uploaded from local, county, and state ME/C Offices and LEAs. Once uploaded, a ten-print search of the postmortem fingerprint record should be performed against the MPI, as well as all criminal and civil records in all available databases—FBI NGI, DHS IDENT, and DoD ABIS. In the event of negative results, a latent-print search of the postmortem fingerprint record should be performed against the MPI, as well as all criminal and civil records in all available databases—FBI NGI, DHS IDENT, and DoD ABIS. In the event of negative ten- and latent-print search results, the postmortem fingerprint record should be retained indefinitely in UDI and continuously searched until the record is identified.

The two agencies most heavily involved in this effort would be the FBI CJIS SPC and the National Missing and Unidentified Persons System (NamUs). NamUs would aid with facilitating retrieval of missing person antemortem fingerprint records from LEAs and families by coordinating fingerprint record requests (where next-of-kin must sign permission for release of records and authorize record upload to MPI) from non-searchable fingerprint repositories or agencies with documentation containing the missing person's fingerprint records (i.e. Department of Motor Vehicles, employment agencies, financial institutions, etc.). Additionally, NamUs would aid with facilitating retrieval of unidentified postmortem fingerprint records from local, county, and state ME/Cs or LEAs that lack resources.

A third index, the Known Deceased Index (KDI), should be populated with postmortem fingerprint records from identified decedents. Currently, known decedent fingerprint records are only retained for a certain time period or expunged following identification. If an individual dies and a postmortem fingerprint record is uploaded and subsequently identified, the postmortem and antemortem fingerprint records are marked as deceased in IAFIS/NGI and cannot be searched against. The record is eventually expunged from the system. If unidentified fingerprints from a cold case crime scene are uploaded and the fingerprints are identical to the fingerprints that were previously marked as deceased, a match will never be made. As such, known deceased fingerprints should be retained and reside in a searchable index within IAFIS/NGI.

The impact of MPI and UDI identifications would affect next-of-kin, as their loved ones would be identified. ME/Cs would be able to close out open and cold unidentified human remains cases. LEAs would be able to close out open and cold missing persons cases, close out active warrants, and gain informational leads for homicide cases. The impact of KDI identifications would aid LEAs with unsolved crime scene samples and allow them to close out open and cold cases, as well as gain informational leads for unsolved crimes.

11.3 OTHER AREAS OF IMPROVEMENT IN POSTMORTEM FINGERPRINTING

Chapter 7 describes in detail how searchable AFIS technologies were created for the purposes of criminal identification. As such, the DEU transaction type described in the same chapter should be modified to allow access and searching of all databases for humanitarian purposes. Also, every transaction should automatically be marked for retention, allowed to contain missing slaps, and forwarded for latent fingerprint searching in the event of negative results following a ten-print search. In addition, the ANSI-NIST standard, as well as state and federal electronic biometric transmission standards (EBTS), restrict specific annotations from being added to the electronic fingerprint records. These standards should be modified to allow for annotations that are specific to postmortem fingerprinting. Furthermore, a standard fingerprint card should be created specifically for postmortem fingerprint processing that allows for multiple fingerprint impressions of the same finger, which are very common during postmortem fingerprint recovery in order to capture as much friction ridge information as possible (explained in detail in Chapter 3).

11.3.1 Research in Postmortem Fingerprint Recovery Techniques

Postmortem fingerprint recovery techniques are continuously advancing due to ongoing research, publications, and information sharing. However, some of the advanced techniques (Figure 11.5a,b) require a significant amount of time, effort, and supplies. As such, continuous research should be pursued in an attempt to develop more efficient and detail-enhancing techniques for severely decomposed remains (Figure 11.6), especially in regards to rehydration of desiccated or mummified fingers, as the Rehydration Technique (explained in detail in Chapter 4) is the most labor-intensive and time-consuming. Streamlined and more efficient postmortem fingerprint recovery techniques will be helpful for large agencies exhibiting a high caseload and during mass fatality incidents, when time and resources are very limited.

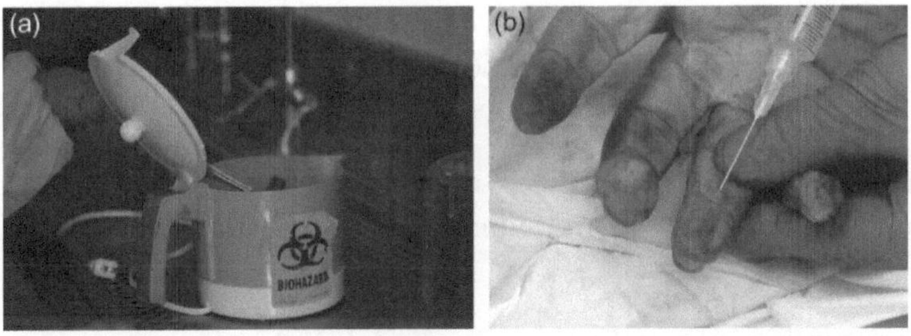

Figure 11.5a,b Use of various advanced postmortem fingerprint recovery techniques (©NYC OCME 2012).

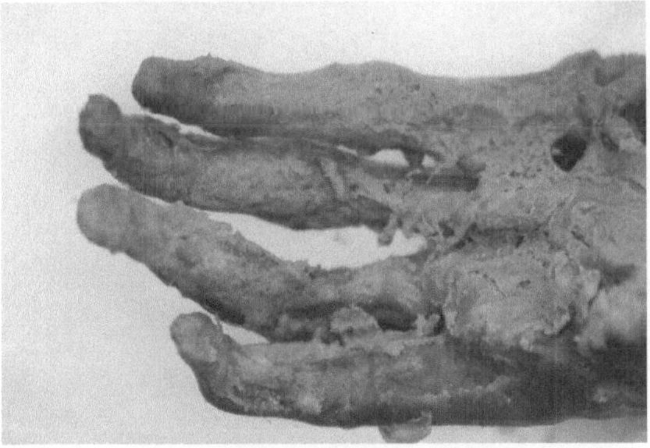

Figure 11.6 Severely decomposed remains (©NYC OCME 2013).

APPENDIX

Fingerprint Records Request Template

Date: [Date]

TO WHOM IT MAY CONCERN:

ME Case No. [Case Number]

Tentative Name: [Last, First Middle] Date of Birth: [DOB]

The [Submitting Agency] is currently investigating the death of the above named decedent and hereby requests a copy of the decedent's fingerprint records, as such records are necessary in order for our agency to fulfill our statutory obligation to identify the decedents, and determine the cause and manner of death in the above case [City/County/State Medical Examiner/Coroner Statute].

Our records indicate this individual was fingerprinted as part of the application process for [Employment Agency, Institution, etc.].

Accordingly, please provide a copy of your fingerprint records for the above individual, preferably in a digital/electronic format. Please fax the fingerprint record to [Fax Number] or email to [Email Address].

Should you require any further information please call the undersigned for further details.

[Signature]

FBI CJIS SPC FINGERPRINT SUBMISSION REQUEST TEMPLATE (CHAPTER 7)

The [Submitting Agency] has an unidentified decedent (DEU Transaction Type). Please see the information below.

Unidentified Deceased Fingerprint Submission	
To:	FBI CJIS SPC spc@leo.gov 304-625-5584 phone 304-625-5587 fax
From:	[Point of Contact] [Submitting Agency] [Email Address] [Phone Number] [Fax Number]
ORI:	[Submitting Agency ORI]
Date:	[mm/dd/yy] [hh:mm] hours [Timezone]
Transaction Type:	Unidentified Deceased (DEU Transaction)
Re:	[Submitting Agency Case #]
Pages:	[#] total ([#] image(s), 1 email)
Comments:	Please attempt to identify this unidentified [gender] who was discovered deceased on [Date of Death mm/dd/yyyy] in [City or County]. Please perform a ten-print search in all available databases (IAFIS/NGI, IDENT, ABIS, etc.) and perform a latent-print search in the event of negative results during a ten-print search. In the event of negative latent-print results, please retain the postmortem fingerprint record in IAFIS/NGI for continuous searching. In advance, thank you for your assistance in the attempt to identify this unidentified person. **NOTE:* *[Special techniques used, if any]* **Please fax fingerprint search results to [Fax Number] or email to [Email Address].**

Use this template for a tentative Missing Person:

Please attempt to identify this unidentified [gender] who was discovered deceased on [Date of Death] in [City or County]. [She/He] may be the missing person, [Missing Person's Name] D.O.B. [mm/dd/yyyy], Social Security # [000-00-0000]. Please compare the attached post-mortem fingerprint records to the ante-mortem fingerprint record of [Mr./Ms. Missing Person's Last Name], if available.

If the decedent is not identified during a comparison of these records, please perform a ten-print search in all available databases (IAFIS/NGI, IDENT, ABIS, etc.) as well as a latent-print search in the event of negative hits during a ten-print search. In the event of negative latent-print results, please retain the postmortem fingerprint record in IAFIS/NGI for continuous searching. In advance, thank you for your assistance in the attempt to identify this unidentified person.

DHS BSC WEST FINGERPRINT SUBMISSION REQUEST TEMPLATE (CHAPTER 7)

The [Submitting Agency] has an unidentified decedent (DEU Transaction Type). Please see the information below.

Unidentified Deceased Fingerprint Submission	
To:	DHS BSC West afis@dhs.gov; lpu@dhs.gov 858-609-2609 phone 858-609-2600 fax
From:	[Point of Contact] [Submitting Agency] [Email Address] [Phone Number] [Fax Number]
ORI:	[Submitting Agency ORI]
Date:	[mm/dd/yy] [hh:mm] hours [Timezone]
Transaction Type:	Unidentified Deceased (DEU Transaction)
Re:	[Submitting Agency Case #]
Pages:	[#] total ([#] image(s), 1 form, 1 email)
Comments:	Please attempt to identify this unidentified [gender] who was discovered deceased on [Date of Death mm/dd/yyyy] in [City or County]. [She/He] may be a foreign national. Please perform a ten-print search in all available databases (IDENT, IAFIS/NGI, etc.) and perform a latent-print search in the event of negative results during a ten-print search. In advance, thank you for your assistance in the attempt to identify this unidentified person. **NOTE: [Special techniques used, if any]* **Please fax fingerprint search results to [Fax Number] or email to [Email Address].**

Use this template for a tentative Missing Person:

Please attempt to identify this unidentified [gender] who was discovered deceased on [Date of Death] in [City or County]. [She/He] may be a foreign national. If the decedent is not identified during a comparison of these records, please perform a ten-print search in all available databases (IDENT, IAFIS/NGI, etc.) as well as a latent-print search in the event of negative hits during a ten-print search. In advance, thank you for your assistance in the attempt to identify this unidentified person.

[She/He] may be the missing person, [Missing Person's Name] D.O.B. [mm/dd/yyyy], Social Security # [000-00-0000]. Please compare the attached post-mortem fingerprint records to the ante-mortem fingerprint record of [Mr./Ms. Missing Person's Last Name], if available.

REFERENCES

Ashbaugh, D. R. (1999). *Quantitative-qualitative friction ridge analysis: an introduction to basic and advanced ridgeology*. Boca Raton: CRC press.

Bauer, L. (2011). *Part two: a coroner's nightmare*. The Kansas City Star <http://www.kansascity.com/2012/05/20/3619904/joplin-coroner-its-about-being.html>.

Biometrics Identity Management Agency (2010). The biometrics triad: working to seamlessly integrate biometric data. *BIMA Newsletter* < http://www.biometrics.dod.mil/Newsletter/issues/2010/Jan/v6issue1_a4.html>.

Biometrics Identity Management Agency (2011). BIMA Annual Report FY11. <http://www.biometrics.dod.mil/Files/Documents/AnnualReports/fy11.pdf>.

Cutro Sr., B. T. (2010). Fingerprint sourcebook-chapter 4: recording living and postmortem friction ridge skin exemplars.

Faulds, H. (1880). On the skin-furrows of the hand. *Nature*, *22*, 605.

Federal Bureau of Investigation, U.S. Department of Justice. The disaster squad serving in the worst of times. <http://www.fbi.gov/news/stories/2010/june/disaster-squad>.

Federal Bureau of Investigation, U.S. Department of Justice. Guidelines for preparation of fingerprint cards and associated criminal history information <http://www.fbi.gov/about-us/cjis/fingerprints_biometrics/guidelines-for-preparation-of-fingerprint-cards-and-association-criminal-history-information>.

Federal Bureau of Investigation, U.S. Department of Justice. Integrated automated fingerprint identification system. <http://www.fbi.gov/about-us/cjis/fingerprints_biometrics/iafis>.

Federal Bureau of Investigation, U.S. Department of Justice. Capturing legible fingerprints <http://www.fbi.gov/about-us/cjis/fingerprints_biometrics/recording-legible-fingerprints/capturing-legible-fingerprints>.

Federal Bureau of Investigation, U.S. Department of Justice (1979). *The science of fingerprints*. Washington, DC: U.S. Government Printing Office.

Federal Bureau of Investigation, U.S. Department of Justice. (2005). Electronic fingerprint transmission specification. <https://www.fbibiospecs.org/docs/efts71.pdf>.

Federal Bureau of Investigation, U.S. Department of Justice. (2008). Biometric interoperability program. <http://www.fbi.gov/about-us/cjis/fingerprints_biometrics/biometric-center-of-excellence/files/fbi_cjis_0208_biometrics>.

Federal Bureau of Investigation, U.S. Department of Justice. (2009). Criminal justice information services division annual report 2009. <http://www.fbi.gov/about-us/cjis/annual-report/cjis_annual_report2009#cjisrp09g>.

Federal Bureau of Investigation, U.S. Department of Justice. (2009). Next generation identification program. <http://www.fbi.gov/about-us/cjis/fingerprints_biometrics/biometric-center-of-excellence/files/fbi_cjis_0209_ngi_onepager020409>.

Federal Bureau of Investigation, U.S. Department of Justice. (2013). Electronic biometric transmission specification. <https://www.fbibiospecs.org/ebts.html>.

Fisher, B. A. (2004). *Techniques of crime scene investigation*. Boca Raton, FL: CRC Press.

Galton, F. (1892). *Finger prints*. London: Macmillan and co.

Galton, F. (1895). *Fingerprint directories*. Macmillan and co.

Gustafson, G. (1966). *Forensic odontology*. London: Staples Press.

Haglund, W. D. (1988). A technique to enhance fingerprinting of mummified fingers. *Journal of Forensic Sciences, 33*(5), 1244.

Hanzlick, R., & Clark, S. (2008). The unidentified decedent reporting system: a model national website registry for the unidentified deceased. *The American Journal of Forensic Medicine and Pathology, 29*(2), 106–113.

Heurich, C. (2008). Cold cases: resources for agencies, resolution for families. *NIJ Journal, 260*, 20–23 <http://www.nij.gov/nij/journals/260/what-is-cold-case.htm>.

Hickman, M. J., Hughes, K. A., Strom, K. J., & Ropero-Miller, J. D. (2007). *Medical examiners and coroners' offices, 2004*. US Department of Justice, Office of Justice Programs, Bureau of Justice Statistics. <http://www.bjs.gov/content/pub/pdf/meco04.pdf>.

Hughes, K. (2007). Unidentified human remains in the United States, 1980–2004. *Electronic document* <http://www.ojp.usdoj.gov/bjs/pub/pdf/uhrus04.pdf> Accessed October, 27 (2013), 1–2.

Kahana, T., Grande, A., Tancredi, D. M., Penalver, J., & Hiss, J. (2001). Fingerprinting the deceased: traditional and new techniques. *Journal of Forensic Sciences, 46*(4), 908–912.

Keiser-Nielsen, S. (1970). Dental identification: Possibilities and difficulties. *Legal Medicine Annual 1970*. New York: Meredith Corporation.

Komarinski, P. (2005). *Automated fingerprint identification systems (AFIS)*. Access Online via Elsevier.

Lauer, M. (2008). A twist of fate. NBC News Dateline Transcript. <http://www.nbcnews.com/id/23849928/#.UoLhEZTF2hN>.

Lee, H. C., Palmbeach, T., & Miller, M. T. (2001). *Henry Lee's crime scene handbook*. London: Academic Press.

Liscio, E. (2013). Forensic uses of 3D printing. *Forensic Magazine*<http://www.forensicmag.com/articles/2013/06/forensic-uses-3d-printing#.UoHMDpTF2hN>.

Marin, N., & Buszka, J. (2013). *Alternate light source imaging: forensic photography techniques*. Anderson Publishing.

May, A. (2008). US-VISIT IDENT Overview. <http://www.cedata.org/cd/HID2010FL/media/m08.swf>.

Miller, R. D. (1995). Recovery of usable fingerprint patterns from damaged postmortem friction ridge skin. *Journal of Forensic Identification, 45*, 602–605.

Modeste, K. I., & Anderson, B. (2009). Using fingerprint powder to record friction ridge details from a Cadaver. *Journal of Forensic Identification, 59*, 302–307.

Moses, K. R. (2011). Automated Fingerprint Identification System (AFIS). Scientific Working Group on Friction Ridge Analysis Study and Technology and National institute of Justice (Eds.) SWGFAST-The fingerprint sourcebook, 1–33.

Mulawka, M. (2010). A uniform protocol to address the rapidly accumulating unidentified human remains and missing persons in united states—A Nation's silent mass disaster. Paper presented at the 62nd Annual Meeting of the American Academy of Forensic Sciences; Seattle, Washington.

Mulawka, M. & Craig, J. (2010a). A study conducted to address the significance of submission of fingerprints obtained from unidentified human remains to various fingerprint databases. Paper presented at the 62nd Annual Meeting of the American Academy of Forensic Sciences; Seattle, Washington.

Mulawka, M. & Craig, J. (2010b). A study conducted to address the significance of submission of fingerprints obtained from unidentified human remains to the department of homeland security biometric support center and the Federal Bureau of investigation criminal justice information services special processing center. Paper presented at the 95th Annual International educational conference of the international association for identification; Spokane, Washington.

Mulawka, M. & DePaolo, F. (2012). Issues with fingerprinting the deceased. Research presented at New York City Office of Chief Medical examiner fingerprint project digital solution focus group meeting; New York City, New York.

Mulawka, M. & DePaolo, F. (2013). The New York City Office of Chief Medical Examiner Fingerprint Project Strategy—A Model Approach for Standardized and Systematic Postmortem Fingerprint Identification. Research presented at the 65th Annual Meeting of the American Academy of Forensic Sciences; Washington, DC.

Mulawka, M., Mosco, M., Uhle, A. & Mokleby, L. (2013). The efficacy of combining various fingerprint acquisition techniques to obtain examination-quality postmortem fingerprints from unidentified human remains. Research presented at the 65th Annual Meeting of the American Academy of Forensic Sciences; Washington, DC.

Mulawka, M., Sebetan, I. M., & Stein, P. (2010). A uniform protocol to address unidentified human remains and missing persons. *Journal of Forensic Identification*, *60*(6), 748–757.

Mulawka, M. H. (2008) A uniform protocol to address the rapidly accumulating unidentified remains and missing persons in the united states – Our Nation's Silent Mass Disaster. Master's Thesis, National University, La Jolla, CA.

Mulawka, M. H., & Craig, J. S. (2011). Efficacy of submitting fingerprint of unidentified human remains to federal agencies. *Journal of Forensic Identification*, *61*(1), 92.

NamUS, (2012): < http://www.untfsu.com/Documents/WyomingNamUsOverview.pdf > .

NamUS, (2013): < http://www.namus.gov/about.htm > .

National Institute of Justice, US Dept Justice, & Office of Justice Programs. (2005). Mass fatality incidents: a guide for human forensic identification. <https://www.ncjrs.gov/pdffiles1/nij/199758.pdf>.

National Institute of Standards and Technology (2000). American National standard for information systems—data format for the interchange of fingerprint, Facial, & Scar Mark & Tattoo (SMT) information. <http://www.nist.gov/itl/ansi/upload/sp500-245-a16.pdf>.

New York State Division of Criminal Justice Services. (2006). DCJS store and forward implementation overview. <http://www.criminaljustice.ny.gov/advtech/overview.pdf>.

New York State Division of Criminal Justice Services. (2007). New York State criminal justice electronic fingerprint transmission standard. <http://criminaljustice.state.ny.us/advtech/efts.pdf>.

Nursall, J. AFIS searching of impressions from charred friction ridge skin. *Journal of Forensic Identification*, *61*(1), 110.

Office of Attorney General, U.S. Department of Justice (2006). The attorney general's report on criminal history background checks. <http://www.justice.gov/olp/ag_bgchecks_report.pdf>.

Pato, J. N., & Millett, L. I. (Eds.), (2010). *Biometric recognition: Challenges and opportunities* National Academies Press.

Paulino, A. A., Jain, A. K., & Feng, J. (2010, August). Latent fingerprint matching: Fusion of manually marked and derived minutiae. In *Graphics, Patterns and Images (SIBGRAPI), 2010 23rd SIBGRAPI Conference on* (pp. 63–70). IEEE. <http://biometrics.cse.msu.edu/Publications/Fingerprint/PaulinoJainFeng_LatentFPMatching_Fusion_SIBGRAPI2010.pdf>.

Pearsall, B., & Weiss, D. (2009). Solving missing persons cases. *National Institute of Justice Journal*, *264*, 4–9 <http://www.nij.gov/journals/264/solving.htm>.

Rice, K. A. (1988). Re-Hydration and printing of mummified fingers. *Journal of Forensic Identification*, *38*(4), 152–156.

Rice, K. A. (1988). Printing of the underside of the epidermal surface of decomposed fingers. *Journal of Forensic Identification*, *38*(3), 98–100.

Rice, K. A. (1992). Printing the deceased who have been subjected to fire. *Journal of Forensic Identification*, *42*(1), 18–25.

Ritter, N. (2007). Missing persons and unidentified remains: the nation's silent mass disaster. *National Institute of Justic Journal, 256*, 7.

Schmidt, C. W., Nawrocki, S. P., Williamson, M. A., & Marlin, D. C. (2000). Obtaining fingerprints from mummified fingers: a method for tissue rehydration adapted from the archeological literature. *Journal of Forensic Sciences, 45*(4), 874–875.

Siwek, D., & Reinecke, G. W. (2014). Relaxation of clenched digits in cadaveric hands to facilitate the recovery of postmortem friction ridge impressions. *Journal of Forensic Identification, 64* (1), 13–17.

Thompson, T., & Black, S. (Eds.), (2010). *Forensic human identification: An introduction* CRC Press.

Tomboc, R., & Schrader, M. (2005). Obtaining fingerprint and palmprint impressions from decomposed bodies or burn victims using the mikrosil casting method. *Journal of Forensic Identification*, *55*(4), 471.

U.S. Department of Homeland Security. Government agencies Using US-VISIT. <http://www.dhs.gov/government-agencies-using-us-visit>.

U.S. Department of Homeland Security (2008). *U.S. Visits Manuals and Standard Operating Procedures*. Washington, DC: U.S. Government Printing Office.

U.S. Department of Homeland Security (2012). DHS Privacy Impact Assessment for the Automated Biometric Identification System (IDENT). <http://www.dhs.gov/sites/default/files/publications/privacy/PIAs/privacy_pia_usvisit_ident_appendixj_jan2013.pdf>.

Uhle, A. J. (2010). Fingerprints and human identification. *Forensic Dentistry,* 79–101. CRC Press.

Uhle, A. J., & Leas, R. L. (2007). The boiling technique: a method for obtaining quality postmortem impressions from deteriorating friction ridge skin. *Journal of Forensic Identification*, *57*(3), 358 <http://www.fbi.gov/about-us/lab/forensic-science-communications/fsc/july2007/index.htm/technical/2007_07_technical01.htm>.

Wagner, G. N. (1997). Scientific methods of identification. *Forensic Dentistry*, 1–36. Boca Raton, FL: CRC Press.

National Institute of Justice, US Department of Justice. (2012). Fingerprint Sourcebook. < https://www.ncjrs.gov/pdffiles1/nij/225320.pdf >.

Western Identification Network (2012). Western identification network service strategy. <http://www.winid.org/winid/what/documents/WINServiceStrategyNovember2012Update.pdf>.

FURTHER READING

BIMA, (2010).Biometrics Identity Management Agency. The biometrics triad: working to seamlessly inte- grate biometric data. BIMA Newsletter < http://www.biometrics.dod.mil/Newsletter/issues/2010/Jan/v6issue1_a4.html >.

Fingerprint Sourcebook, (2010). National Institute of Justice, US Department of Justice. (2012). Fingerprint Sourcebook. < https://www.ncjrs.gov/pdffiles1/nij/225320.pdf >.

National Academies report, Strengthening Forensic Science in the United States (2009): National Research Council. (2009). Strengthening Forensic Science in the United States: A Path Forward.